500
salads

500
salads

Susannah Blake

APPLE

A Quintet book

First published in the UK in 2010 by
Apple Press
7 Greenland Street
London NW1 0ND
United Kingdom

www.apple-press.com

ISBN: 978-1-84543-352-9
QTT.FHSA

This book was conceived, designed and produced by
Quintet Publishing Limited
6 Blundell Street
London N7 9BH
United Kingdom

Project Editor: Martha Burley
Editorial Assistants: Camilla Barton, Tanya Laughton
Food Stylist: Liz Martin
Photographer: Michael Dannenberg
Designer: Tania Field
Art Director: Michael Charles
Managing Editor: Donna Gregory
Publisher: James Tavendale

10 9 8 7 6 5 4 3 2

Printed in China by 1010 Printing International Ltd.

Shutterstock images appear on pages 7, 11, 12, 15, 16 and 21.

contents

introduction

Salads are incredibly versatile and come in a seemingly endless array of colours, shapes and sizes. Whether you're looking for a side dish or a filling main meal, a healthy snack, a wholesome lunch, a luxurious and indulgent treat smothered with creamy dressing or a luscious, fruity dessert, there's always a salad that's just perfect for you.

Most often thought of as a cold dish, salads can also be served warm – featuring fresh greens topped with hot or warm grilled poultry or fish, or perhaps tossed in a warm dressing just before serving. They can be light and leafy, consisting primarily of one of the many salad greens now available at most large supermarkets, or hearty and wholesome, based on cooked rice, pasta or beans. Salads can be a whole meal-in-one, with meat, poultry, fish or shellfish, eggs, tofu or another protein, or they can be an appetiser course, whetting the appetite for the meal to come.

Salads are perfect for almost any occasion. Sweet, fruity salads such as blueberry and papaya salad with toasted almonds (page 264) are wonderful for breakfast, brunch or as a dessert, while a lighter salad such as watercress and apple salad with chicory and bacon (page 53) can be a delicious choice for an appetiser. There are simple healthy salads that will appeal to children, such as two-tone coleslaw (page 177), and more sophisticated salads, like warm duck salad with honey–orange dressing (page 106). There are the classic salads of different cuisines, whether it's cucumber salad with yoghurt and dill from Eastern Europe (page 41), tuna sashimi salad from Asia (page 246), Middle Eastern fattoush (page 25), insalata caprese from Italy (page 39) or cobb salad from the US (page 32). And there are all those main-dish salads featuring a good balance of nutrients, vegetables, carbohydrates (such as pasta, rice, potatoes or bread) and protein (such as chicken, meat, fish, shellfish, tofu, eggs or cheese).

equipment

Although you can make most salads using the most basic of kitchen equipment, there are a few essentials, plus a few handy extras, that will make salad-making easy.

salad spinner

Salad leaves should be washed thoroughly to remove any dirt, grit or other debris. It's drying the leaves that's tricky, because they're so easily crushed or damaged. Invest in a salad spinner, which will remove the water from the leaves, leaving them clean and dry and ready for use.

chopping board

A basic chopping board comes in handy for slicing and chopping lettuces, vegetables and fruit, as well as other ingredients such as grilled chicken breasts, cheese and hard-boiled eggs.

knives

A basic chef's knife is suitable for most salad-making needs. A serrated knife greatly simplifies slicing ingredients such as tomatoes.

mandolines, slicers & graters

A mandoline will come in handy for recipes that require very thinly sliced ingredients, such as cucumber or carrots. A specially designed cheese slicer is useful for shaving off thin slices of cheese, but it also can be used to slice cucumber thinly. An egg slicer that allows you to cut a hard-boiled egg into even slices in one motion can come in handy. Graters are great for shredding cucumber, carrots and other root vegetables such as beetroots and cheese.

vegetable peeler

Useful for peeling potatoes, carrots and fruit such as apples and pears, a vegetable peeler can also be used to pare thin slices of carrot for salads, or shavings of Parmesan or Pecorino to scatter over the top.

bowls & servers

Although many salads can be served individually, a large salad bowl is always invaluable – either for serving or for combining and tossing ingredients together. Smaller bowls can be used for mixing up salad dressings, and for holding prepared ingredients such as snipped herbs or sliced vegetables before combining and serving. Two large spoons are needed for tossing salads and serving.

whisk or jar with screw-top lid

Although most dressings can be whisked together in a small bowl with a small whisk, it is even easier to put all your ingredients into a screw-top jar and shake together.

ingredients

There's no limit to the type or quantity of ingredients you can put in a salad. You're likely to use lettuce or some type of salad greens, but even these aren't essential. Here are some ideas.

salad greens

There are countless types of salad greens, all with their own distinct taste, texture and appearance, and all providing a great base for salads. Some, such as iceberg or Romaine, are far more common than others, but look more closely at the produce section of your supermarket or shop at a farmer's market to find some of the more unusual varieties. Iceberg, green- or red-leaf lettuce and baby spinach leaves will give you a mildly flavoured salad, while nutty rocket leaves, peppery watercress, chicory, escarole (also known as Batavian endive) and radicchio will add a distinctive, stronger flavour. A cellophane bag of mixed greens is ideal for many uses, providing different coloured, shaped and flavoured leaves for maximum impact.

vegetables

Lots of vegetables, raw or cooked, are great in salads. Not only do they add extra nutrients, but they also add huge visual appeal with their various bright colours. Classic raw ingredients include cucumber, carrot, tomato, onion, bean sprouts, peppers, celery and avocado. However, cooked ingredients – added warm or cold – can make a great addition too. Try roasted peppers, squash, red onions, cherry tomatoes and cooked beetroot, or lightly blanched broccoli, cauliflower and green beans. Cold, cooked new potatoes are a great addition to salads and can help transform a light accompaniment into a main meal.

fruits

Fresh fruits such as pear, apple, grapes, peaches or nectarines, kiwi fruit, oranges, grapefruit and berries can make a great addition to savoury salads, providing a sweet, juicy tang. Fruits can also be used as the base of dessert salads and are delicious in most combinations. Select a few different fruits with different flavours, textures and colours – such as apple, orange and blueberry, or pineapple, mango and strawberry – and simply peel or slice into bite-sized pieces and toss with a splash of fruit juice or dessert wine.

beans, pasta & grains

Adding hearty pasta, beans, or grains to a salad can be a great way of boosting nutrients and turning a light salad into a substantial one. All three provide plenty of healthy carbohydrates for energy, but beans contain lots of fibre and protein too. Whole grains such as brown rice and bulgur wheat are a good source of fibre, while some such as quinoa are a powerhouse of nutrients containing protein as well.

proteins

Meat, poultry, fish, egg, cheese and tofu are all delicious in savoury salads. They are good combined with salad greens, pasta, grains or beans and are made even more delicious with the addition of salad vegetables, fruits and herbs.

additions & embellishments

Adding little finishing touches to a salad, whether it's a handful of crunchy croûtons or a sprinkling of cheese, can transform a simple salad into something much more luxurious. Try some of these classic finishing touches.

herbs

Fresh herbs can make a fabulous addition to both sweet and savoury salads, adding flavour as well as colour. Fresh mint is particularly good in fruit salads, but it works well in savoury salads too, for example in tabbouleh. Fragrant basil is especially well suited to tomatoes and Mediterranean-style salads, while fresh coriander is a popular ingredient in Asian-style salads. Chives go well with egg, cheese and potato-based salads, while dill is a classic flavouring for fish. Feel free to experiment according to taste, but be careful when using strongly flavoured herbs such as rosemary, as their flavour can become overpowering.

edible flowers

Many flowers are edible and make a stunning addition to salads. Most herb flowers are pretty and will add a lovely taste to salads, while other edible flowers include rose petals, nasturiums, lavender, violets, pansies and courgette flowers.

croûtons

Crisp croûtons can add a delicious crunch to savoury salads. Buy them ready-made from the supermarket or make your own. To make them, remove the crusts from thick-sliced white bread, cut the bread into cubes, then place on a baking sheet and drizzle with olive oil (or a flavoured oil such as garlic or chilli oil). Toss the cubes to ensure they are evenly coated, then bake at 200°C (400°F/Gas mark 6) for about 7 minutes until crisp and golden.

cheese

All kinds of cheeses are good for embellishing a salad, but particularly good ones include Parmesan; Pecorino (either grated finely or cut into fine shavings using a vegetable peeler); crumbled blue cheese or feta; or strips of grilled halloumi.

nuts

Nuts are a good source of protein and can add a delicious flavour and texture when sprinkled – either whole or roughly chopped – over a savoury or sweet salad just before serving. Try toasting nuts such as pine nuts, peanuts, cashews, pistachios and hazelnuts first. To toast, heat them in a dry frying pan, tossing over the heat for a few minutes, just until golden. Keep a close eye on them as they can easily burn, which will spoil their flavour.

seeds

Like nuts, seeds are highly nutritious and can add a lovely crunch and flavour to salads. Pumpkin and sunflower seeds are great sprinkled over most savoury salads, while tiny sesame and poppy seeds are good in grated carrot salads and coleslaw. Pumpkin, sunflower and sesame seeds can be toasted in the same way as nuts to bring out their flavour.

dressing ingredients

Often adding a splash or drizzle of dressing is the final touch that transforms a salad from something good to something sensational. There are countless dressings from sweet and scented ones to sharp and tangy, rich and creamy, spicy, light or aromatic, but most start by combining a sharp liquid such as vinegar or lemon juice with an oil, plus other flavourings to enhance the combination. Choosing the vinegar and the oil for your salad is generally a matter of personal taste.

Olive oil, with its distinctively rich, fruity flavour, is a classic used in dressings. For the best results, choose extra-virgin olive oil obtained from the first olive pressing. For some salads, a good-quality olive oil can be used on its own as a dressing – for example, a simple tomato, mozzarella and basil salad only needs a little seasoning and a drizzle of olive oil to be enjoyed at its best.

Oils such as canola, sunflower and grapeseed have a much milder flavour and are great for dressings that carry other, stronger tastes such as herbs, mustard and honey, or even stronger Asian-style aromatics such as garlic, ginger and chilli pepper.

Balsamic vinegar is rich, dark and sweet. It's great for making full-bodied dressings. The dark colour of the dressing is often particularly good for drizzling and looks stunning over a fresh, brightly coloured salad served on a white plate.

White and red wine vinegars, as well as sherry and cider vinegars, have a light, fresh flavour on their own and also combine well with other classic dressing ingredients such as mustard, honey, garlic and herbs.

Fruit vinegars usually have a wine vinegar base so they have the same characteristics, but often with a fruity hint. Raspberry is a particularly popular fruit vinegar.

Lemon juice is one of the classic souring ingredients used for dressings. It has a light, very sharp flavour, so dressings made with lemon juice often benefit from the addition of a little sugar or honey.

favourite dressings

There are hundreds of different dressings that are all delicious, and depending on which one you choose, you can transform the whole character of a salad. They can be light and zesty, rich and creamy, fresh and fruity or tart and tangy. Those described below are absolute classics and are good drizzled over a simple leaf salad, as well as over more complex pasta, bean, grain and vegetable salads.

asian-style dressing

Stir together 175 ml (6 fl. oz) rice wine vinegar, 2 tablespoons sugar, ½ deseeded and finely chopped red chilli pepper and 1 tablespoon chopped fresh coriander until the sugar has dissolved. Season with Thai fish sauce to taste. Alternatively, place the ingredients in a screw-top jar and shake together to combine.

balsamic dressing

Whisk together 2 tablespoons balsamic vinegar, 4 tablespoons olive oil and salt and freshly ground black pepper to taste. Alternatively, place the ingredients in a screw-top jar and shake together to combine.

blue cheese dressing

Blend briefly in a food processor or blender 100 g (4 oz) mayonnaise, 100 g (4 fl. oz) soured cream, 75 g (3 oz) crumbled blue cheese, 1½ teaspoons white wine vinegar and a good grinding of black pepper until smooth and creamy.

caesar salad dressing
Whisk together 100 g (4 oz) mayonnaise, 1 tablespoon Dijon mustard, 1 crushed anchovy fillet, ½ crushed garlic clove, 1½ tablespoons olive oil and ½ tablespoon white wine vinegar. Season with ground black pepper.

honey–mustard dressing
Whisk together (or shake in a screw-top jar) 1 tablespoon Dijon mustard, 1 tablespoon honey, ½ crushed garlic clove, 2 tablespoons cider vinegar, 5 tablespoons canola oil and a good grinding of black pepper.

simple french dressing
Whisk together (or shake in a screw-top jar) 2 tablespoons white wine vinegar, a pinch of sugar, a pinch of salt, a good grinding of black pepper and 5 tablespoons olive oil.

sun-dried tomato dressing
Whisk (or shake) together 2 tablespoons red wine vinegar, 2 finely chopped sun-dried tomatoes in olive oil, a pinch of sugar, a pinch of salt, a good grinding of black pepper and 5 tablespoons oil from the sun-dried tomato jar.

thousand island dressing
Stir together 100 g (4 oz) mayonnaise, 1 tablespoon tomato ketchup, a good splash of Worcestershire sauce, 1 tablespoon chopped parsley, 1 tablespoon snipped chives and ground black pepper to taste.

classic salads

There are so many salads to choose from, but it's often the classics that you can't help picking, again and again. This chapter brings the old favourites, such as Caesar salad, chef's salad and Greek salad, right back into focus by adding a modern, irresistible twist.

fattoush

see variations page 42

Serve this classic Middle Eastern salad, made of chopped tomatoes, cucumber and flatbread, for a light lunch or supper or a delicious accompaniment.

juice of ½–1 lemon
2–3 large, ripe tomatoes, in bite-sized pieces
½ cucumber, diced
2 stalks fresh basil, roughly chopped
¼ bunch fresh parsley, roughly chopped

for the toasted bread:
flatbread (approx. 400 g/14 oz), such as pitta bread
roughly 50 ml (2 fl. oz) olive oil
sea salt and pepper

Mix the lemon juice with the tomatoes and cucumbers. Add the chopped herbs and toss to combine.

Dice the bread, put into a bowl and sprinkle with olive oil. Mix well so that all the pieces are wet with oil. Put the bread on a baking sheet and toast in a preheated oven 160°C (325°F/Gas mark 3) for about 10 minutes, or until crisp and golden. Leave the toasted bread to cool slightly before mixing with the salad. Sprinkle with sea salt and pepper and serve.

Serves 2

caesar salad

see variations page 43

Here's the ultimate recipe for a classic Caesar salad. Feel free to add your own personal touch to make a new classic recipe!

3 large cloves of crushed garlic
175 ml (6 fl. oz) extra virgin olive oil
3 thick slices of stale white bread, crusts removed
2 medium-size heads romaine lettuce
salt and freshly ground black pepper
1 tsp Worcestershire sauce
50 ml (2 fl. oz) fresh lemon juice
2 tbsp ready-made mayonnaise
6 anchovies, drained and finely chopped
75 g (3 oz) Parmesan, grated

Bruise the garlic with a heavy knife or rolling pin, and cover with olive oil. Marinate for 1 hour. Cut the bread into 2-cm (¾-in) cubes. Remove the garlic from the oil and set aside. Toss the bread cubes with 4 tablespoons of oil, and bake for 20 minutes at 150°C (300°F/ Gas mark 2), turning to toast evenly.

Remove the outer leaves of the lettuce. Tear the remaining leaves into 5 cm (2 in) pieces and place in a salad bowl. Season with salt and pepper and toss with the remaining garlic-flavoured oil. Mix together the Worcestershire sauce, lemon juice and mayonnaise. Pour over the lettuce and toss. Add the croûtons and anchovies and toss again. Sprinkle with grated Parmesan and serve.

Serves 6

frisée salad with blue cheese & bacon

see variations page 44

Salty bacon and tangy blue cheese are a classic combination, particularly in salads, and go together wonderfully here to create a light and flavoursome meal.

12 thin slices baguette
1 head frisée (or curly endive)
4 bacon slices
100 g (4 oz) blue cheese, crumbled

for the dressing:
6 tbsp olive oil
4 tbsp sherry vinegar (or balsamic vinegar)
salt and freshly ground pepper

Toast the baguette slices under the grill until golden brown on both sides.

Wash the frisée, spin-dry and tear into bite-sized pieces. Arrange on plates. Cut the bacon into thirds and sauté in a dry non-stick frying pan until crisp and brown. Remove and drain.

To make the dressing, whisk together the olive oil and sherry vinegar. Season with salt and pepper.

Scatter the cheese over the lettuce. Drizzle with dressing, scatter with bacon and serve with the toasted baguette slices.

Serves 4

potato salad with mayonnaise–yoghurt dressing

see variations page 45

Potato salad, a favourite with everyone, is perfect for family meals, barbecues and buffets. This version uses a tangy mayonnaise–yoghurt dressing in place of the more classic mayonnaise.

1 kg (2¼ lb) waxy white potatoes
2 spring onions
for the dressing:
4 tbsp white wine vinegar
175 g (6 oz) mayonnaise
75–100 g (3–4 oz) natural yoghurt
salt and freshly ground pepper
chopped fresh chives, to garnish

Wash the potatoes and cook in boiling, salted water for 25–30 minutes. Drain, leave to steam dry, then peel and slice while still hot.

Wash and trim the spring onions and cut into thin rings.

Mix the vinegar, mayonnaise, yoghurt, salt and pepper to make a dressing. Allow the potatoes to cool down slightly, then mix them with the dressing while they are still warm. Leave the salad to cool completely, stirring from time to time. Either stir the spring onions in carefully or scatter over the top with the fresh chives before serving.

Serves 4

cobb salad

see variations page 46

This great salad has a little bit of everything, making it a whole meal in a bowl. The first Cobb salad was created by Bob Cobb, manager of Hollywood's Brown Derby Restaurant in the 1920s or 1930s.

6 slices bacon
2 boneless, skinless chicken breasts
salt and freshly ground pepper
1 avocado
2 tbsp lemon juice
1 small head lettuce (bibb or iceberg), torn
1 small head of radicchio, torn
100–175 g (4–6 oz) tinned corn kernels, drained
2 medium-size ripe tomatoes, sliced
2 hard-boiled eggs, sliced
1 red onion, cut into rings
2 tbsp freshly chopped watercress, to garnish

for the dressing:
4 tbsp oil
2 tbsp white wine vinegar
1 tsp strong mustard
2 tbsp chicken stock
1 tsp honey
salt and freshly ground pepper

Fry the bacon in a dry frying pan until crisp and brown. Remove and drain on kitchen towel. Season the chicken breasts with salt and pepper. Fry on all sides in the bacon fat for 8–10 minutes, or until cooked through. Remove, drain and leave it to cool.

Peel and halve the avocado, remove the stone and cut into wedges. Sprinkle with lemon juice. Arrange the lettuce, radicchio, corn, tomatoes, eggs, avocado and onion rings attractively on 4 plates. Mix the dressing ingredients, check the seasoning and pour over the salad. Slice the chicken and add to the plate. Scatter with roughly crumbled bacon. Serve sprinkled with watercress.

Serves 4

chef's salad with thousand island dressing

see variations page 47

Everyone loves a hearty, wholesome chef's salad and this one, with its creamy and tangy thousand island dressing, certainly won't disappoint.

for the dressing:
1 gherkin
1 shallot
2 hard-boiled eggs
½ red pepper
scant 50 g (2 oz) mayonnaise
3 tbsp double cream
3 tbsp tomato ketchup
salt to taste
chilli powder, to taste

for the salad:
2 boneless, skinless chicken breasts
1 head lettuce
175 g (6 oz) cooked ham
1 ripe tomato
4 hard-boiled eggs
75 g (3 oz) grated Emmental or Swiss cheese
50 g (2 oz) Milano salami, sliced

To make the dressing, finely chop the gherkin. Peel and grate the shallot. Remove the yolks from the eggs (use the whites for another purpose) and push through a sieve. Put the pepper into a hot oven until the skin blisters, then pull off the skin and chop the pepper very finely. Mix the gherkin, shallot, yolks and pepper with the mayonnaise, cream and tomato ketchup. Add salt and chilli powder to taste. Pour the dressing into a small serving bowl.

Season the chicken breasts with salt and chilli powder and cook in a steamer for about 8–10 minutes, or until done. Leave to cool, then cut into strips.

Divide the head of lettuce into leaves, wash and spin-dry. Cut the ham into strips. Quarter the tomatoes; remove the core, pulp and seeds; and cut each quarter into 4 strips. Peel the hard-boiled eggs and cut into eighths. In a large bowl, toss the lettuce, ham, tomato, eggs, cheese and sliced salami. Serve on individual salad plates and pass the dressing separately.

Serves 4

apple & celery salad with walnuts & parmesan

see variations page 48

A twist on the classic Waldorf salad, this crisp, crunchy salad with sweet–tangy apple, wholesome walnuts, and a creamy, flavoursome dressing is hard to beat.

2 apples, thinly sliced
3 stalks celery, thinly sliced
1 fennel bulb, thinly sliced (use mandoline if available)
4 tbsp chopped walnuts
50 g (2 oz) freshly shaved Parmesan
for the dressing:
2 tbsp mayonnaise
1 tbsp Cognac
1 tbsp tomato ketchup
scant 50 g (2 oz) natural yoghurt
2 tbsp lemon juice
cayenne pepper, to taste
salt and freshly ground black pepper, to taste
2 tbsp nut oil (or canola oil)

Loosely mix the sliced apples, celery and fennel in a large bowl, then arrange on 4 plates. Scatter walnuts and Parmesan shavings over each serving.

To make the dressing, mix the mayonnaise with the Cognac, tomato ketchup, yoghurt and lemon juice. Season to taste with salt and cayenne pepper. Drizzle the dressing over the salad and sprinkle with freshly ground pepper. Add a few drops of nut oil and serve immediately.

Serves 4

insalata caprese

see variations page 49

An Italian classic, and perfect for serving as an appetiser, you'll never get bored with the fabulous combination of sweet red tomatoes, creamy white mozzarella and fragrant green basil leaves.

2 tbsp virgin olive oil
2 tbsp lemon juice
salt and freshly ground pepper
2 medium-size ripe tomatoes, sliced
225 g (8 oz) mozzarella, sliced
small bunch fresh basil, to garnish

Mix the oil, lemon juice, salt and pepper.

Arrange the tomato and mozzarella slices in a fan shape in small dishes and sprinkle with the dressing. Serve garnished with basil leaves.

Serves 2

greek salad

see variations page 50

This classic salad is refreshing, tangy and perfect for serving as an accompaniment at a barbecue, or as a meal-in-one with chunks of crusty baguette.

½ cucumber, peeled, deseeded and diced
1 green pepper, cut into strips
2 medium-size ripe tomatoes, diced
1 red onion, sliced into rings
1 romaine lettuce heart, torn in bite-sized pieces
1 tbsp black olives, pitted and halved
1 tbsp green olives, pitted and halved
1 clove garlic, finely chopped
150 g (5 oz) feta cheese, diced

for the dressing:

4 tbsp olive oil
2 tbsp wine vinegar
1 tsp capers
pinch of sugar
salt and freshly ground pepper
2 tbsp chopped fresh basil, to garnish

Toss together the cucumber, pepper, tomatoes, onion, lettuce, olives, garlic and cheese in a serving bowl.

To make the dressing, mix the olive oil with the vinegar, capers, sugar, salt and pepper. Pour the dressing over the salad and toss to combine. Add more salt and pepper to taste, if desired. Carefully stir the chopped basil into the salad before serving.

Serves 2

cucumber with yoghurt & dill

see variations page 51

Variations of this classic cucumber and yoghurt salad are enjoyed in numerous countries countries including Turkey, Greece, Eastern Europe and India.

1 large cucumber
1 small onion
175 g (6 oz) low-fat natural yoghurt
75–100 ml (3–4 fl. oz) double cream
salt and freshly ground pepper
fresh dill torn into small pieces, to garnish

Peel the cucumber and slice lengthways into long ribbons using a mandoline vegetable slicer or a vegetable peeler. Pile loosely in 4 bowls. Put into the freezer for up to 30 minutes, until just beginning to freeze.

Meanwhile, roughly chop the onion and put it into a blender or food processor with the yoghurt and cream. Blend until smooth. Season with salt and pepper.

Take the cucumber out of the freezer, pour the yoghurt dressing on top and serve garnished with dill.

Serves 4

variations

fattoush

see base recipe page 24

fattoush with black olives
Prepare the basic recipe, adding 100 g (4 oz) black olives to the tomatoes and cucumbers.

hot & spicy fattoush
Prepare the basic recipe, stirring 1 teaspoon harissa into the lemon juice before combining with the tomatoes and cucumbers.

fattoush with green pepper
Prepare the basic recipe, adding 1 deseeded, diced green pepper to the tomatoes and cucumber.

fattoush with fresh mint
Prepare the basic recipe, adding 1½ tablespoons chopped fresh mint with the parsley.

variations

caesar salad

see base recipe page 26

chicken caesar salad

Prepare the basic recipe, adding 2 sliced, grilled chicken breasts to the leaves and toss with the Parmesan and dressing.

red hot caesar salad

Prepare the basic recipe, adding half a deseeded and finely chopped red chilli to the dressing.

caesar salad with chicken and cashew nuts

Prepare the basic recipe, tossing 2 sliced grilled chicken breasts and a generous handful of toasted cashew nuts into the salad before tossing with the Parmesan and dressing.

caesar salad with sweet chilli tofu

Marinate 350 g (12 oz) tofu (cut into 1-cm/½-in dice) in 1½ tablespoons sweet chilli sauce and 2 tablespoons soy sauce. Fry in a hot frying pan with 1 tablespoon of oil until golden. Prepare the basic recipe and add to the salad and toss with the Parmesan and dressing.

variations

frisée salad with blue cheese and bacon

see base recipe page 28

frisée salad with feta cheese & cherry tomatoes
Prepare the basic recipe, replacing the blue cheese with the same quantity of crumbled feta cheese. Omit the bacon, and instead scatter 225 g (8 oz) halved cherry tomatoes over the salad with the cheese.

frisée salad with goat's cheese & bacon
Prepare the basic recipe, replacing the blue cheese with the same quantity of diced goat's cheese.

spinach salad with blue cheese & bacon
Prepare the basic recipe, using 4 large handfuls of baby spinach leaves in place of the frisée.

spinach salad with blue cheese & grapes
Prepare the basic recipe, using 4 large handfuls of baby spinach leaves in place of the frisée. Omit the bacon, and instead scatter 225 g (8 oz) halved seedless grapes over the salad with the cheese.

rocket salad with blue cheese & bacon
Prepare the basic recipe, using 4 large handfuls of rocket leaves in place of the frisée lettuce.

variations

potato salad with mayonnaise–yoghurt dressing

see base recipe page 30

potato salad with fragrant herb dressing
Prepare the basic recipe, adding 1 tablespoon each of snipped fresh chives, finely chopped fresh dill and chopped fresh flat-leaf parsley to the dressing.

potato salad with green olives
Prepare the basic recipe, adding 175 g (6 oz) halved and pitted green olives to the potatoes before tossing with the dressing.

potato salad with lemon dressing
Prepare the basic recipe, stirring the finely grated zest of 1 lemon into the dressing before tossing with the potatoes.

potato salad with mustard dressing
Prepare the basic recipe, stirring 2 teaspoons wholegrain mustard into the dressing before tossing with the potatoes.

potato salad with chopped egg
Prepare the basic recipe, sprinkling the salad with 1 chopped hard-boiled egg before serving.

variations

cobb salad

see base recipe page 32

vegetarian cobb salad

Prepare the basic recipe, omitting the chicken and bacon and add 4 sliced hard-boiled eggs instead of 2.

cobb salad with seeds

Prepare the basic recipe, and sprinkle the salad with 1 tablespoon pumpkin seeds and 1 tablespoon sunflower seeds before serving.

tuna cobb salad

Prepare the basic recipe, omitting the chicken and bacon. Instead, drain a 200-g (7-oz) tin tuna, then flake the fish over the salad before dressing and sprinkling with watercress.

mixed vegetable salad

Prepare the basic recipe, omitting the chicken, bacon and egg.

variations

chef's salad with thousand island dressing

see base recipe page 34

swiss cheese salad with thousand island dressing
Prepare the basic recipe, omitting the chicken, ham and salami.

ham salad with thousand island dressing
Prepare the basic recipe, omitting the chicken, grated cheese and salami.

chicken salad with thousand island dressing
Prepare the basic recipe, omitting the ham, grated cheese and salami.

chef's salad with raspberry vinaigrette
Prepare the basic recipe, using raspberry vinaigrette dressing (page 63) in place of the thousand island dressing.

chef's salad with honey–orange dressing
Prepare the basic recipe, using honey–orange dressing (page 106) in place of the thousand island dressing.

variations

apple & celery salad with walnuts & parmesan

see base recipe page 36

apple & fennel salad with pecans & parmesan
Prepare the basic recipe, omitting the celery and using chopped pecans in place of the walnuts.

apple & celery salad with hazelnuts & manchego
Prepare the basic recipe, using coarsely chopped hazelnuts in place of the walnuts, and shavings of manchego in place of the Parmesan.

pear & celery salad with walnuts & parmesan
Prepare the basic recipe, using ripe but firm pears in place of the apples.

rocket, apple & celery salad
Prepare the basic recipe. Place a handful of rocket leaves on each plate before topping with the salad.

simple apple & celery salad
Prepare the basic recipe, using 6 celery stalks in place of the original celery and fennel. In place of the dressing, use 6 tablespoons mayonnaise.

variations

insalata caprese

see base recipe page 38

avocado, mozzarella & tomato salad
Prepare the basic recipe, adding 1 peeled, pitted and sliced avocado to the tomato and mozzarella fan.

mozzarella & tomato salad with balsamic dressing
Prepare the basic recipe, using 1½ tablespoons balsamic vinegar in place of the lemon juice.

insalata caprese with garlic toasts
Prepare the basic recipe. Toast 4 slices of ciabatta until golden. Cut a garlic clove in half and rub the cut side over the toasts, then drizzle with olive oil and serve with the salads.

mozzarella & tomato salad with watercress
Prepare the basic recipe, omitting the basil. Instead, place a small handful of watercress leaves on each plate and arrange the salad on top.

variations

greek salad

see base recipe page 40

mediterranean olive salad
Prepare the basic recipe, omitting the feta cheese.

tomato & feta salad
Prepare the basic recipe, omitting the cucumber and green pepper and using 4 tomatoes instead of 2.

cucumber & feta salad
Prepare the basic recipe, using 1 whole cucumber in place of the half, and omitting the tomatoes.

tomato & red onion salad
Prepare the basic recipe omitting the cucumber, and using 1½ red onions and 4 tomatoes.

variations

cucumber with yoghurt & dill

see base recipe page 41

cucumber salad with yoghurt & mint
Prepare the basic recipe, using 1 tablespoon chopped fresh mint in place of the dill.

cucumber salad with yoghurt & coriander
Prepare the basic recipe, using 2½ tablespoons chopped fresh coriander in place of the dill.

grated cucumber & yoghurt salad
Prepare the basic recipe, but rather than freezing and slicing the peeled cucumber, grate it coarsely and leave it to drain in a colander for about 30 minutes.

cucumber salad with spring onion
Prepare the basic recipe, replacing the onion with 6 sliced spring onions.

light & healthy salads

Crunchy fresh salad greens, zesty dressings and nutrient-packed ingredients such as nuts, seeds, fish and brightly coloured fruits and vegetables are brought together in these recipes to create a fantastic choice of light and healthy salads.

watercress & apple salad with chicory & bacon

see variations page 77

The combination of slightly bitter greens with salty bacon, sharp apple and sweet maple dressing is absolutely perfect in this light, tasty salad.

175 g (6 oz) watercress
1 head chicory, leaves separated
4 thick-cut bacon slices (or 5 regular slices)
1 apple, cored and cut into wedges
1 tbsp pure maple syrup
3 tbsp balsamic vinegar
4 tbsp grapeseed oil (or canola oil)
salt and freshly ground pepper

Put a bed of watercress on each salad plate. Arrange the chicory leaves attractively on the watercress.

Cut each slice of bacon into thirds, then fry in a dry frying pan until crisp and brown. Remove bacon from the pan and allow to drain on kitchen towel. Fry the apple wedges in the bacon fat on both sides until golden brown. Remove and drain on kitchen towel.

Mix the maple syrup with the balsamic vinegar and oil, then season to taste with salt and pepper. Sprinkle the dressing over the salad. Scatter the fried bacon and apple wedges on top and serve.

Serves 4

organic bean sprout salad

see variations page 78

This simple, light, healthy salad is a great accompaniment to any meal. It makes a perfect choice to serve at a barbecue with grilled meat or fish.

1 carrot
700 g (1½ lb) mixed organic bean sprouts
3 tbsp apple cider vinegar
2 tbsp nut oil (or canola oil)
salt

Peel and finely grate the carrot. Mix the carrot with the sprouts, vinegar and oil, and season to taste with salt.

Serves 4

green salad with red cabbage & grapefruit

see variations page 79

Serve this light, refreshing salad with its bitter tang of grapefruit as an appetiser or an accompaniment to grilled fish or chicken.

2 grapefruit
1 tbsp honey
3 tbsp nut oil (or canola oil)
salt and freshly ground pepper
1 head oak-leaf lettuce, in bite-sized pieces
1/4 head red cabbage, shredded
1 cucumber, halved lengthways and sliced thin
2 tbsp sunflower seeds
2 tbsp pumpkin seeds

Finely grate the zest of 1 grapefruit. Then peel both grapefruit, remove the white pith and membrane and cut into segments, avoiding the membrane. Work over a bowl to catch the juice. Squeeze the trimmings into the bowl.

Mix the grapefruit juice with the honey and nut oil, and season to taste with salt and pepper.

Arrange the lettuce, red cabbage, grapefruit pieces and cucumber on serving plates. Scatter each serving with the seeds and grapefruit zest. Sprinkle the dressing over each plate and serve.

Serves 4

mixed leaf salad with fennel & orange

see variations page 80

Fresh, sweet, zesty orange is the perfect partner for thinly sliced crisp fennel with its distinctive anise flavour. Serve this simple salad as an appetiser or accompaniment.

2 oranges
1 fennel bulb
for the dressing:
3 tbsp sherry vinegar (or balsamic vinegar)
1 tsp honey
1/2 tsp hot mustard
3 tbsp sunflower oil (or canola oil)
salt and freshly ground pepper
275 g (10 lb) mixed salad greens, torn in bite-sized pieces
1 red onion, thinly sliced
fresh dill, to garnish

Peel the oranges and cut off the white pith using a sharp knife. Cut out the orange segments, collecting any orange juice in a small bowl. Squeeze the juice from the remaining pulp into the bowl. Wash and clean the fennel, quarter it and remove the hard core. Shred the fennel into fine slices.

To make the dressing, add the vinegar, honey and mustard to the orange juice and mix. Slowly drizzle in the oil and mix until it is well combined. Season with salt and pepper.

Arrange the salad greens, fennel slices, onion slices and orange segments on salad plates. Drizzle each serving with the dressing. Serve garnished with dill.

Serves 4

escarole & chicory salad with blood oranges

see variations page 81

Deep-red blood oranges help to create a stunning salad that's great for serving as an appetiser or accompaniment to grilled meat such as lamb kebabs.

1 small head escarole (Batavian endive)
1 head chicory
2 blood oranges
100g (4 oz) natural yoghurt
2 tbsp. crème fraîche
3 tbsp apple cider vinegar
1 tbsp honey
salt and freshly ground pepper
2 tbsp capers

Wash and sort the escarole and chicory, and coarsely shred the larger leaves. Arrange on individual salad plates.

Peel the blood oranges with a sharp knife, removing all the white pith. Cut out segments, avoiding the membrane. Catch any juice and squeeze the fruit trimmings. Mix together the orange juice with the yoghurt, crème fraîche, vinegar and honey. Season to taste with salt and pepper.

Scatter the orange segments and capers over the escarole and chicory. Drizzle with the dressing before serving.

Serves 4

pear salad with walnuts & roquefort

see variations page 82

This light and refreshing pear salad, with its raspberry vinaigrette dressing, makes a wonderfully simple yet sophisticated salad for a dinner party or special meal.

1 bunch rocket
1 bunch watercress or garden cress
4–5 tbsp roughly chopped walnuts
100 g (4 oz) Roquefort cheese, crumbled
2 ripe pears

for the vinaigrette:
1 clove garlic, finely chopped
6 tbsp olive oil
4 tbsp raspberry vinegar
½–1 tbsp honey
salt and freshly ground pepper

Wash and dry the rocket and watercress and remove the stalks. Rip leaves into pieces and place in a serving bowl. Sprinkle with the chopped walnuts. Sprinkle half of the Roquefort into the bowl.

To make the vinaigrette, whisk the garlic with the olive oil and raspberry vinegar. Season to taste with honey, salt and pepper. Pour the vinaigrette over the greens and mix well.

Peel the pears and remove the core. Quarter the pears or cut into slices. Put the pears in the bowl with the salad and toss gently. Arrange the salad on plates, sprinkle the remaining Roquefort over the top and serve.

Serves 4

spinach salad with strawberries & macadamia nuts

see variations page 83

Fresh berries are a great addition to leafy green salads, adding a distinctive sweet–sharp flavour and lovely juicy texture.

1 cucumber
350 g (12 oz) fresh young spinach, washed and dried
2 cups quartered strawberries
175 g (6 oz) shelled macadamia nuts
1 tbsp whole-grain Dijon mustard
1 tbsp honey
3 tbsp white wine vinegar
3 tbsp grapeseed oil (or canola oil)
salt and freshly ground pepper
½ bunch fresh chervil, to garnish

Peel the cucumber, halve lengthways, scrape out the seeds and dice the flesh. Put into a serving bowl with the spinach, strawberries and macadamia nuts.

Mix the mustard with the honey, vinegar and oil. Season to taste with salt and pepper. Add the dressing to the serving bowl and toss. Check the seasoning and serve scattered with chervil leaves.

Serves 4

mixed vegetable salad with strawberries

see variations page 84

This simple vegetable and fruit salad is delicious served as an accompaniment to grilled fish, chicken and meat. Make it in summer when strawberries are at their best.

1 tbsp oil
1 tbsp butter
1 small onion, very finely diced
1 clove garlic, very finely diced
4–6 tbsp white balsamic vinegar
1 yellow pepper, cut in strips
½ cucumber
1 small head of lettuce, torn into bite-sized pieces
350 g (12 oz) fresh strawberries, quartered
shredded fresh basil
fresh lemon balm leaves, to garnish

Heat the oil and butter in a small pan and sauté the onion and garlic until translucent. Stir in the vinegar and add the pepper. Leave to cool.

Thinly slice the cucumber, using a mandoline vegetable slicer if available. In a large bowl, mix the lettuce with the cucumber, strawberries and basil. Add the onion and pepper dressing and toss to combine. Serve in bowls garnished with lemon balm.

Serves 4

chopped tomato salad with scallions

see variations page 85

This simple salad makes a fabulous accompaniment to any meal, but it's also great piled up on slices of toasted baguette as bruschetta.

25 ml (1 fl. oz) white wine vinegar
salt and white pepper
scant 50 ml (2 fl. oz) olive oil
6 ripe plum tomatoes, diced
2 spring onions, cut into rings

Mix the vinegar with salt and pepper and gradually whisk in the olive oil.

Mix the tomatoes with the spring onions and put on plates. Drizzle with the dressing before serving. Serve with freshly baked bread.

Serves 2

celery & orange salad with black olives

see variations page 86

Crisp, crunchy celery is a great addition to raw vegetable salads. Here, with sweet, tangy, juicy bits of orange, it's lovely.

450 g (1 lb) sliced celery (or celeriac)
4 oranges
juice of 1/2 lemon
100 g (4 oz) natural yoghurt
2 tbsp grapeseed oil (or canola oil)
salt and freshly ground pepper
50 g (2 oz) chopped black olives, to serve

Blanch the celery in boiling, salted water for about 2 minutes. Refresh in cold water and drain.

Peel the oranges, removing all the white pith and membrane. Cut out the segments, avoiding the membrane. Dice the orange segments. Squeeze the fruit trimmings, then mix the orange juice with the lemon juice, yoghurt and oil. Season with salt and pepper as needed. Mix the orange pieces and celery with the dressing and put into glasses. Serve with chopped olives.

Serves 4

chicory & radicchio salad with mandarin oranges & seeds

see variations page 87

The combination of bitter salad leaves and sweet, juicy oranges is just divine in this simple but sophisticated salad.

175 g (6 oz) torn lettuce leaves
1 small head radicchio, torn
2 heads chicory, separated into individual leaves
2 mandarin oranges, divided into segments
100 g (4 oz) halved seedless grapes

for the dressing:
4 tbsp favourite vinegar
4 tbsp favourite oil
½ tsp honey
salt and freshly ground pepper
1 tbsp each of peanuts, pumpkin seeds and sunflower seeds

Put the lettuce, radicchio, chicory, oranges and grapes in a large bowl. Toss to combine.

To make the dressing, mix the vinegar with the oil, honey, salt and pepper. Taste and adjust the seasoning as desired. Pour the dressing over the salad and toss. Transfer the salad to individual plates and scatter each serving with the nuts and seeds.

Serves 4

green leaf salad with edible flowers

see variations page 88

Edible flowers make a stunning and delicious addition to salads. They are particularly suitable for meals for special occasions.

for the dressing:
3 tbsp white wine vinegar
1 tsp raspberry vinegar
$^{1}/_{2}$ tsp mustard
pinch of sugar
salt and freshly ground pepper

for the salad:
5 tbsp corn (or canola) oil
roughly 100 g (4 oz) edible flowers (such as mallows, pansies, nasturtiums, carnations, borage, marigolds or chrysanthemums)
350 g (12 oz) mixed salad greens, torn in bite-sized pieces

Mix the vinegars with the mustard, sugar, salt and pepper. Whisk in the oil and set aside.

Wash the flowers if necessary, shake dry and pat dry carefully.

Put the salad greens into a salad bowl. Add the dressing and toss well. Scatter the flowers over the salad and serve.

Serves 4

salmon & vegetable salad in a cucumber cup

see variations page 89

These pretty, light, refreshing salads served wrapped in a slice of cucumber make a stunning appetiser for a special meal.

2 small cucumbers
salt
4–6 leaves green or red loose-leaf lettuce
1 apple, cut into 12 wedges
1 carrot, cut into long, thin sticks
1 pear, cut into long, thin sticks
1 avocado, cut into wedges
200 g (7 oz) smoked salmon
8 chives

Wash the cucumbers and peel 8 or so thin slices lengthways from each one. Use the outer slices and the middles (the pieces with a lot of seeds) for another purpose (such as a salad). Lay 12 slices side by side and sprinkle with salt.

Wash the lettuce leaves and shake dry. Divide each leaf into 2–3 pieces, discarding the central vein. To make the cucumber rolls, lay a slice of cucumber on a working surface, top with an apple wedge, a few carrot and pear sticks, a slice of avocado, a little lettuce and a slice of smoked salmon. Roll up. Tie with a chive. Stand the roll upright on a plate. Repeat with the other cucumber slices.

Serves 4

variations

watercress & apple salad with chicory & bacon

see base recipe page 53

watercress & pear salad with chicory and bacon
Prepare the basic recipe, using 1 pear in place of the apple. Peel and core the pear before slicing.

watercress & apple salad with chicory & sun-dried tomato
Prepare the basic recipe, omitting the bacon slices. Instead, thinly slice 5 sun-dried tomatoes in oil and sprinkle them over the salad before serving.

watercress, apple & celery salad
Prepare the basic recipe, replacing the chicory with 4 sliced celery stalks.

watercress & apple salad with chicory & walnuts
Prepare the basic recipe, omitting the bacon slices. Instead, scatter 50 g (2 oz) walnut pieces over the salad before serving.

variations

organic bean sprout salad

see base recipe page 54

super-sprout & seed salad
Prepare the basic salad, adding 1 tablespoon each of pumpkin seeds, poppy seeds and sesame seeds.

spicy bean sprout salad
Prepare the basic recipe, whisking together the vinegar and oil with 1 tablespoon sweet chilli sauce before tossing with the salad.

gingery bean sprout salad
Prepare the basic recipe, whisking together the vinegar and oil with 1 teaspoon freshly grated root ginger before tossing with the salad.

bean sprout salad with blueberries
Prepare the basic recipe, tossing in 175 g (6 oz) fresh blueberries with the bean sprouts and grated carrot.

bean sprout & hazelnut salad
Prepare the basic recipe, sprinkling 3 tablespoons toasted chopped hazelnuts over the salad before serving.

variations

green salad with red cabbage & grapefruit

see base recipe page 56

green salad with red cabbage & orange
Prepare the basic recipe, replacing the 2 grapefruit with 3 large oranges. Use the grated zest of 1 orange.

green salad with grapefruit & avocado
Prepare the basic recipe, replacing the red cabbage with 2 handfuls of rocket leaves. Arrange the sliced flesh of 2 peeled, pitted avocados on the salad with the grapefruit and cucumber.

green salad with red cabbage, grapefruit & parmesan
Prepare the basic salad, omitting the sunflower and pumpkin seeds and topping the salad with shavings from 25 g (1 oz) fresh Parmesan.

green salad with grapefruit, red cabbage & pistachios
Prepare the basic recipe, using 3 tablespoons chopped and toasted pistachio nuts in place of the sunflower and pumpkin seeds.

green salad with red cabbage & apples
Prepare the basic recipe, using 3 sliced, cored apples in place of the grapefruit and 4 teaspoons white wine vinegar in the dressing in place of the grapefruit juice.

variations

mixed leaf salad with fennel & orange

see base recipe page 58

mixed leaf salad with fennel, orange & black olives
Prepare the basic recipe, scattering 175 g (6 oz) pitted black olives over the salad before dressing.

mixed leaf salad with fennel, orange & parsley
Prepare the basic recipe, sprinkling 3 tablespoons freshly chopped flat-leaf parsley over the salad in place of the dill.

mixed leaf salad with fennel, orange & watercress
Prepare the basic recipe, using 4 large handfuls of watercress leaves in place of the mixed salad greens.

mixed leaf salad with fennel, orange & spring onions
Prepare the basic recipe, using 5 sliced spring onions in place of the red onion.

mixed leaf salad with fennel, orange & avocado
Prepare the basic recipe, adding 2 peeled, pitted, diced avocados to the salad plates.

variations

escarole & chicory salad with blood oranges

see base recipe page 60

escarole, chicory & orange salad with tiger prawns
Prepare the basic recipe, adding 275 g (10 oz) cooked and peeled tiger prawns (or jumbo shrimp) to the salad with the orange segments.

escarole, chicory & orange salad with artichokes
Prepare the basic salad, adding 6 bottled marinated artichoke hearts to the salad with the orange segments.

escarole, chicory & orange salad with poppy seeds
Prepare the basic recipe, sprinkling 2 tablespoons poppy seeds over the salad before serving.

escarole, chicory & orange salad with blueberries
Prepare the basic recipe, scattering 2 handfuls of fresh blueberries over the salad with the orange segments.

escarole, chicory & orange salad with chickpeas
Prepare the basic recipe, scattering 400 g (14 oz) tinned, drained and rinsed chickpeas over the salad with the orange segments.

variations

pear salad with walnuts & roquefort

see base recipe page 62

baby spinach salad with pear & roquefort
Prepare the basic recipe, using 4 large handfuls of baby spinach leaves in place of the rocket and watercress.

rocket, pear & parmesan salad
Prepare the basic recipe, replacing the watercress with an extra bunch of rocket, and the Roquefort with shavings of 25 g (1 oz) of Parmesan.

pear salad with walnuts & parma ham
Prepare the basic recipe, using 6 strips of Parma ham, torn into bite-sized pieces, in place of the Roquefort.

nectarine salad with walnuts & roquefort
Prepare the basic recipe, using 3 pitted, sliced nectarines in place of the pears.

spinach salad with strawberries & macadamia nuts

see base recipe page 64

spinach salad with raspberries & pistachios

Prepare the basic recipe, using raspberries in place of the strawberries and toasted shelled pistachio nuts in place of the macadamia nuts.

spinach salad with peaches & pine nuts

Prepare the basic recipe, using 3 sliced, pitted peaches in place of the strawberries and 3 tablespoons toasted pine nuts in place of the macadamia nuts.

rocket salad with strawberries & hazelnuts

Prepare the basic recipe, using rocket leaves in place of the spinach and 75 g (3 oz) toasted hazelnuts in place of the macadamia nuts.

watercress salad with strawberries & macadamia nuts

Prepare the basic recipe, using watercress leaves in place of the spinach.

herb salad with strawberries & macadamia nuts

Prepare the basic recipe, omitting the chervil. Instead, add a small handful each of coriander leaves, 2 tablespoons chopped fresh dill and a small handful of fresh basil leaves.

variations

mixed vegetable salad with strawberries

see base recipe page 66

mixed vegetable salad with blueberries
Prepare the basic recipe, using blueberries in place of the strawberries.

mixed vegetable salad with cherries
Prepare the basic recipe, using pitted cherries in place of the strawberries.

mixed vegetable salad with raspberries
Prepare the basic recipe, using raspberries in place of the strawberries.

mixed vegetable salad with kiwi fruit
Prepare the basic recipe, using 4 peeled kiwi fruit cut into bite-sized pieces in place of the strawberries.

chopped tomato salad with spring onions

see base recipe page 68

chopped tomato & basil salad

Prepare the basic recipe, adding a small handful of torn basil leaves in place of the spring onions.

chopped tomato & mozzarella salad

Prepare the basic recipe, adding 1 mozzarella ball (about 100 g/4 oz), torn into bite-sized pieces, with the tomatoes.

chopped tomato & sweet pepper salad

Prepare the basic recipe, replacing the 6 tomatoes with 1 deseeded and diced yellow pepper and 4 tomatoes.

chopped tomato salad with balsamic vinegar

Prepare the basic recipe, using 2 tablespoons balsamic vinegar in place of the white wine vinegar.

spicy chopped tomato salad

Prepare the basic recipe, whisking ½ deseeded, finely chopped green chilli pepper into the dressing.

variations

celery & orange salad with black olives

see base recipe page 70

celery & orange salad with walnuts
Prepare the basic recipe, using a handful of walnut pieces in place of the black olives.

fennel & orange salad with black olives
Prepare the basic recipe, using 2 large, finely sliced fennel bulbs in place of the celery.

celery & pear salad with black olives
Prepare the basic recipe, using 4 pears, cut into bite-sized wedges, in place of the oranges, and stir 2 tablespoons orange juice into the dressing.

celery & apple salad with black olives
Prepare the basic recipe, using 4 cored apples, cut into bite-sized chunks, in place of the oranges and stir 2 tablespoons orange juice into the dressing.

celery, orange & peach salad with black olives
Prepare the basic recipe, using 3 oranges and 2 peaches (pitted and cut into wedges) in place of the original 4 oranges. Stir 2 tablespoons orange juice into the dressing.

chicory & radicchio salad with mandarin oranges & seeds

see base recipe page 72

chicory & radicchio salad with pears
Prepare the basic recipe, using 2 sliced pears in place of the oranges.

chicory, radicchio & orange salad with pecorino cheese
Prepare the basic recipe, omitting the nuts and seeds, and instead scattering shavings from 25 g (1 oz) Pecorino cheese over the finished salad.

chicory, radicchio & orange salad with poppy seeds
Prepare the basic recipe, using 1 tablespoon poppy seeds in place of the peanuts, pumpkin seeds and sunflower seeds.

chicory & radicchio salad with plums
Prepare the basic recipe, replacing the oranges with 4 pitted plums cut into bite-sized wedges.

chicory, beet & orange salad
Prepare the basic recipe, using 1 extra head of chicory in place of the radicchio and adding 2 cooked (not in vinegar) sliced beetroots with the oranges.

variations

green leaf salad with edible flowers

see base recipe page 74

green leaf & cucumber salad with edible flowers
Prepare the basic recipe, scattering ¼ cucumber, thinly sliced, over the leaves with the flowers.

green leaf & herb salad with edible flowers
Prepare the basic recipe, scattering 3 tablespoons chopped mixed herbs (such as parsley, chives and mint) over the salad leaves before adding the flowers and dressing.

green leaf salad with grapes & edible flowers
Prepare the basic recipe, scattering 225 g (8 oz) halved seedless grapes over the salad with the flowers.

green leaf salad with blueberries & edible flowers
Prepare the basic recipe, scattering 225 g (8 oz) fresh blueberries over the salad with the flowers.

variations

salmon & vegetable salad in a cucumber cup

see base recipe page 76

salmon, vegetable & mango salad in a cucumber cup
Prepare the basic recipe, using 1/2 pitted, peeled mango in place of the pear.

salmon, vegetable & peach salad in a cucumber cup
Prepare the basic recipe, using 1 pitted peach in place of the pear.

salmon, vegetable & dill salad in a cucumber cup
Prepare the basic recipe, sprinkling the carrot, apple and pear with a little fresh dill before rolling up.

salmon, vegetable & coriander salad in a cucumber cup
Prepare the basic recipe, sprinkling the carrot, apple and pear with 1/2 teaspoon chopped fresh coriander before rolling up.

warm salads

Simple salads made warm with the addition of grilled meat, poultry or fish, or perhaps a drizzle of hot dressing, offer a tantalising twist to the classic chilled or cool salad. They're great served throughout the year – whether it's warm or cool outside.

warm lentil salad

see variations page 109

Firm lentils such as brown and Puy lentils make the ideal base for salads as they retain their shape once cooked. This salad is great served warm or cold.

275 g (10 oz) brown lentils
¼ cucumber
1 cup small cherry tomatoes, quartered
5 radishes, cut into small sticks
2 carrots, finely diced
2 spring onions, finely chopped
1 red onion, finely diced
1 tbsp finely chopped fresh parsley
for the dressing:
2 tbsp safflower oil (or canola oil)
4 tbsp apple cider vinegar
salt and freshly ground pepper
purslane (stems removed) and small salad leaves, to serve

Place the lentils in a large saucepan, cover with salted water and bring to the boil. Turn heat to medium-low, cover and simmer about 30–40 minutes or until tender. Drain well.

Peel the cucumber, halve lengthways, scrape out the seeds and finely dice the flesh. In a large bowl, mix the cucumber with the lentils, tomatoes, radishes, carrots, spring onions and onion. Add the chopped parsley.

Make a dressing from the safflower oil, vinegar, salt and pepper. Pour the dressing over the lentil salad and mix well. Serve the salad on plates on a bed of purslane and lettuce leaves.

Serves 4

warm goat's cheese & spinach salad

see variations page 110

Spinach, bacon and goat's cheese are a classic combination. When the goat's cheese is warm and melting, as it is here, it's especially delicious.

300 g (11 oz) goat's cheese
4 slices baguette
8 slices bacon
1 tbsp honey
juice of 1 lemon
3 tbsp olive oil
2 tbsp pine nuts
salt and freshly ground pepper
2 handfuls baby spinach

Slice the goat's cheese into 4 equal slices. Toast the slices under a preheated grill for 2–3 minutes, or until golden brown. Toast the baguette slices for about 1 minute per side, or until nicely browned. Fry the bacon in a frying pan until crisp; drain on kitchen towels.

Meanwhile, mix the honey with the lemon juice, the olive oil and the pine nuts. Season to taste with salt and pepper.

Arrange spinach on each plate, then add bacon and a slice of toasted baguette. Put the warm, toasted cheese on the baguette, sprinkle with dressing and serve immediately.

Serves 4

potato, chorizo & rocket salad

see variations page 111

Hot and spicy Spanish chorizo sausage gives a meaty bite to this warm fried-potato salad. Serve as a light lunch or supper or a hearty appetiser.

2 potatoes
100 g (4 oz) chorizo, cut into slices
1 red onion, halved, and thinly sliced
2 tbsp balsamic vinegar
2 tbsp olive oil
1 bunch rocket, tough stalks removed
salt and freshly ground pepper
1 pinch dried ground coriander
freshly grated Parmesan, to serve

Peel the potatoes and cook for about 20 minutes in salted water until tender. Drain and leave to cool. Cut into quarters or eighths, depending on the size.

Sauté the chorizo in a hot frying pan, add the onion slices and potatoes and continue to fry until golden brown. Remove from the heat.

Mix the balsamic vinegar and the olive oil together in a bowl. Add the rocket and season with salt and pepper. Now add the warm chorizo, potato and onion mixture, and gently toss together. Season with coriander and arrange on plates. Serve with freshly grated Parmesan.

Serves 2

cooked vegetable salad with basil

see variations page 112

Lightly cooked Mediterranean vegetables tossed with fresh basil leaves and served while still warm make a delicious meal accompaniment or a simple appetiser served with chunks of crusty bread.

700 g (1½ lb) fresh, ripe tomatoes, sliced
olive oil, for sprinkling and frying
salt and freshly ground pepper
1 carrot, peeled and sliced
400 g (14 oz) baby artichokes, trimmed and halved
4 cloves garlic, finely chopped
225 g (8 oz) pearl onions, peeled
175 ml (6 fl. oz) white wine
175 ml (6 fl. oz) chicken stock
100 g (4 oz) pitted, halved green olives
1 bunch fresh basil, roughly chopped

Put the tomatoes on a baking tray lined with waxed paper or parchment paper, and sprinkle with olive oil. Season with salt and pepper and grill under a preheated grill for 1–2 minutes per side. Remove.

In a medium-size, ovenproof frying pan, heat a little olive oil. Sauté the carrot and artichokes. Add the garlic and onions, then stir in the white wine and stock. Cook until the carrot and artichokes are tender (or your desired firmness) and the liquid is almost evaporated. Stir in the olives, cook briefly to warm through. Brown quickly under the grill, if you wish.

Put all the cooked vegetables into a salad bowl with the chopped basil and a little oil if necessary. Season to taste with salt and pepper and serve immediately.
Serves 4

warm sweet potato salad

see variations page 113

Zesty ginger, spicy cayenne pepper and fragrant coriander are the perfect match for tender, buttery sweet potatoes in this simple, warming salad. The toasted macadamia nuts add a delightful crunch.

1 kg (2¼ lbs) sweet potatoes, peeled and diced
350 g (12 oz) macadamia nuts
175 ml (6 fl. oz) vegetable stock
3 tbsp white balsamic vinegar
3 tbsp sunflower oil (or canola oil)
1 tbsp honey
1 tsp freshly grated root ginger
salt and cayenne pepper to taste
1 bunch fresh coriander

Cook the sweet potatoes in salted water for about 10 minutes, or until tender. Drain well.

Toast the nuts in a dry, non-stick frying pan.

Mix the stock with the balsamic vinegar, oil, honey and ginger. Add the potatoes and nuts and toss gently. Season with salt and cayenne pepper and leave to cool slightly. Pick off the coriander leaves and mix into the salad. Check the seasoning and serve.

Serves 4

aubergine salad with pomegranate seeds, herbs & feta

see variations page 114

Salty, crumbly feta and smoky, smooth aubergine make the perfect flavour combination in this Greek-inspired salad.

3 small–medium aubergines
5 tbsp olive oil, plus more for brushing
salt and freshly ground pepper
1 pomegranate
juice of 2 lemons
1 clove garlic
sprigs of fresh parsley
sprigs of fresh mint
175 g (6 oz) crumbled feta cheese

Wash the aubergines and cut into approximately 1-cm (½-in) thick slices. Sprinkle with salt and leave to stand for about 15 minutes. Then rinse with cold water and pat dry with kitchen towels. Brush the slices on both sides with some olive oil and season with salt and pepper. Grill on both sides under a hot grill until golden brown.

Meanwhile, slice the pomegranate and carefully remove the seeds. Mix 5 tablespoons olive oil with the lemon juice. Press the garlic into the oil and lemon juice dressing and stir to combine. Sprinkle the warm aubergine slices with the dressing, toss and leave to stand for 2–3 minutes. Pick the leaves from the parsley and mint sprigs and mix with the aubergine slices. Season to taste with salt and pepper. Put the aubergine salad on a platter, sprinkle with pomegranate seeds, scatter with crumbled feta cheese and serve.

Serves 4

marinated vegetable carpaccio

see variations page 115

Traditionally carpaccio is made of thinly sliced raw beef, veal or tuna, marinated with garlic, olive oil and other flavourings. Here, vegetables are marinated in a similar way to make a delicious salad that's perfect as a starter.

2 courgettes
3 carrots
2 tbsp sunflower oil (or canola oil)
1 garlic clove, chopped
2 tbsp olive oil
3 tbsp white balsamic vinegar
1 tbsp capers
1 bunch fresh mint
salt and freshly ground pepper
dash of lemon juice

Wash and trim the courgettes and slice thinly at an angle. Peel and thinly slice the carrots, also at an angle, using a mandoline vegetable slicer if available.

Heat the sunflower oil in a frying pan and sauté the carrots and courgettes until golden brown. Add the garlic at the end. Remove and drain on a kitchen towel.

Put the vegetables into a bowl with the olive oil, balsamic vinegar and capers and mix. Chop the mint (reserving a few leaves to garnish) and add to the vegetables. Season with salt and pepper, add lemon juice to taste and leave at room temperature to marinate for at least 3 hours. Check the seasoning before serving.

Serves 4

marinated leek salad

see variations page 116

This cold salad of tender, cooked leeks drenched in a zesty coriander marinade makes a wonderful accompaniment to chicken or fish, or piled onto toast as a snack.

2 stalks celery, sliced
1 bunch coriander, roughly chopped
75–100 ml (3–4 fl. oz) grapeseed oil (or canola oil)
3 tbsp balsamic vinegar
juice of ½ lemon
salt and freshly ground pepper
3 tbsp olive or canola oil
4 leeks, cut into 7.5-cm (3-in) lengths

In a medium mixing bowl, mix the sliced celery, chopped coriander, grapeseed oil, balsamic vinegar and lemon juice. Season with salt and pepper. Set aside.

Heat the oil in a large frying pan. Add the leeks and slowly sauté over a low to medium heat until golden brown. Remove from heat and add to the celery-coriander marinade. Toss to mix, then marinate for at least 3 hours. Season to taste before serving.

Serves 4

rocket salad with sliced duck breast

see variations page 117

This elegant salad makes a wonderful starter for a special dinner party or a light supper or lunch served with chunks of crusty bread.

2 cloves garlic
¼ tsp cayenne pepper
6 tbsp olive oil
2 boneless, skinless duck breasts (each weighing about 285 g/10½ oz)
salt and freshly ground pepper

for the dressing:
½ tsp hot mustard
4 tbsp balsamic vinegar
1–2 bunches fresh rocket
275 g (10 oz) cherry tomatoes, cut into wedges, to serve
35 g (1½ oz) wedge of Parmesan, to serve

Peel and press the garlic. Mix the garlic with the cayenne pepper and 2 tablespoons olive oil. Rub the duck breasts on all sides with this mixture, cover and leave to stand for 1 hour.

Put the duck breasts skin-side down in a hot frying pan and fry over a medium heat for about 8 minutes. Turn over and fry for 3 more minutes. Season with salt and pepper, wrap in aluminium foil and put in a very low oven for about 20 minutes to rest. Remove from the oven and leave to cool slightly.

Mix the mustard with the balsamic vinegar, salt and pepper. Whisk in the rest of the oil and check the seasoning.

Wash and sort the rocket, spin dry and arrange on 4 plates with the tomatoes. Sprinkle with the vinaigrette. Slice the duck breasts at an angle, then arrange the slices on top of the rocket. Shave the Parmesan with a vegetable peeler and scatter over the salad.

Serves 4

warm duck salad with honey–orange dressing

see variations page 118

Duck and orange are a classic combination. This zesty honey–mustard dressing flavoured with orange juice is wonderful drizzled over strips of pan-fried duck and nutty rocket leaves.

1–2 whole beetroot (about 150 g/5 oz), depending on the size)
225 g (8 oz) rocket, tough stems removed
2 ripe mangos, peeled, pitted and cut into 1-cm (½-inch) cubes
2 tbsp freshly chopped chives
salt and freshly ground pepper
400 g (14 oz) boneless, skinless duck breasts
2 tbsp oil
4 tbsp freshly chopped parsley
2 tbsp pumpkin seeds or sunflower seeds

for the dressing:
½ clove garlic, finely chopped
2 tbsp freshly squeezed orange juice
1½ tsp Dijon mustard
1 tsp honey
¾ tsp salt
100 ml (4 fl. oz) olive oil
salt and freshly ground pepper

Wash the beetroot. Remove the roots and the stalk. Wrap each beetroot in aluminium foil and cook in a preheated oven at 180°C (350°F/Gas mark 4) for 1 hour until tender. Leave to cool, peel and cut into 1-cm (½-in) cubes.

Mix the garlic with the orange juice, mustard, honey and salt. Slowly drizzle the olive oil into the dressing, stirring constantly, until it forms a creamy sauce. Season with salt and pepper. Mix 3 tablespoons of the dressing with the beetroot cubes.

For the salad, place the rocket in a bowl. Add two-thirds of the mango cubes. Add the chives and 5 tablespoons of the dressing and mix well. Season with salt and pepper and arrange on plates.

Cut the duck breasts into strips and season with salt and pepper. Heat the oil in a frying pan, add the duck strips and fry until done to your preference. Remove the duck from the pan and mix with the parsley and 6 tablespoons dressing. Arrange the duck strips on top of the salads. Divide the marinated beetroot cubes and the remaining mango cubes over the salads. Garnish with pumpkin or sunflower seeds and serve.

Serves 4

warm potato & egg salad

see variations page 119

This warm and colourful potato and egg salad is rich with the flavour of herbs and piquant shallot and makes a great choice for a buffet or barbecue.

400 g (14 oz) firm-cooking potatoes
100 ml (4 fl. oz) vegetable stock
1 shallot, finely diced
100 g (4 oz) chopped radishes
1 tbsp snipped fresh chives
1 tbsp chopped fresh dill
1 tbsp mayonnaise
3 tbsp wine vinegar
2 tbsp sunflower oil (or canola oil)
2 hard-boiled eggs, chopped
salt and freshly ground pepper

Wash the potatoes, then steam in their skins for about 30 minutes, or until cooked. Peel, leave to cool slightly and slice.

In a saucepan, bring the vegetable stock to the boil. Add the diced shallot. Remove from the heat and pour over the potato slices. Mix in the radishes, herbs, mayonnaise and vinegar. Finally, carefully stir in the oil and chopped eggs and season to taste with salt and pepper. Best served at room temperature

Serves 2

variations

warm lentil salad

see base recipe page 91

warm lentil & spinach salad

Prepare the basic recipe, tossing 2 handfuls of baby spinach leaves into the lentils with the parsley.

warm lentil & new potato salad

Prepare the basic recipe. Quarter 8 new potatoes and steam for about 10 minutes, or until tender. Add the potatoes to the salad with the tomatoes.

warm lentil & herb salad

Prepare the basic recipe, replacing the tablespoon of parsley with 3 tablespoons roughly chopped fresh coriander leaves and 2 tablespoons roughly chopped fresh parsley leaves.

warm lentil & poached egg salad

Prepare the basic recipe. Poach 4 eggs in barely simmering water, then lift out of the water, drain on kitchen towel and serve warm, one on top of each plate.

warm lentil & broccoli salad

Prepare the basic recipe. Divide 225 g (8 oz) broccoli into florets and steam for about 4 minutes until just tender. Toss into the salad with the tomatoes and other vegetables.

variations

warm goat's cheese & spinach salad

see base recipe page 92

honeyed warm goat's cheese & spinach salad
Prepare the basic recipe, drizzling each slice of cheese with 1 teaspoon honey before grilling.

warm goat's cheese & spinach salad with roasted peppers
Prepare the basic recipe, omitting the bacon. Instead, slice 4 roasted peppers (from a jar). Scatter the pieces over the spinach before adding the baguette and goat's cheese.

warm goat's cheese, spinach & kiwi salad
Prepare the basic recipe, scattering bite-sized pieces of 4 peeled kiwis over the salad with the bacon.

warm goat's cheese & spinach salad with pistachio nuts
Prepare the basic recipe, sprinkling 3 tablespoons roughly chopped toasted and shelled pistachios over the salad in place of the pine nuts.

variations

potato, chorizo & rocket salad

see base recipe page 94

potato, chorizo & rocket salad with cherry tomatoes
Prepare the basic recipe, tossing a generous 100 g (4 oz) halved cherry tomatoes into the salad with the fried chorizo, potatoes and onion.

spicy potato & rocket salad
Prepare the basic recipe, omitting the chorizo. Fry the onion and potato as before, but add a good pinch of crushed dried chilli flakes.

potato, chorizo & frisée salad
Prepare the basic recipe, using about half a head of frisée (curly endive) lettuce in place of the rocket.

potato, chorizo & herb salad
Prepare the basic recipe, replacing the rocket and coriander with mixed salad leaves, 1 tablespoon snipped fresh chives, 1 tablespoon chopped fresh dill and 2 tablespoons chopped fresh coriander.

potato, kabanos & rocket salad
Prepare the basic recipe, using Polish kabanos sausage in place of the chorizo.

variations

cooked vegetable salad with basil

see base recipe page 95

cooked vegetable salad with basil & rocket
Prepare the basic recipe. Arrange a large handful of rocket on each serving plate, then spoon the salad on top to serve.

cooked vegetable salad with basil & toasted pine nuts
Prepare the basic recipe, adding 4 tablespoons toasted pine nuts with the basil.

cooked vegetable & couscous salad with basil
Prepare the basic recipe. Meanwhile, put 175 g (6 oz) couscous in a bowl and stir in 1 tablespoon olive oil and a good pinch of salt. Cover with 225 ml (8 fl. oz) boiling water and leave to stand for 5 minutes. Fluff up the couscous and toss with the cooked vegetables and fresh basil.

cooked vegetable & fusilli salad with basil
Cook 225 g (8 oz) fusilli in salted boiling water according to the packet instructions, then drain and rinse in cold water. Prepare the basic recipe, then toss the pasta with the cooked vegetables and fresh basil leaves.

cooked vegetable & flageolet bean salad with basil
Prepare the basic recipe, tossing two 400-g (14-oz) tins flageolet beans (drained and rinsed) with the cooked vegetables and fresh basil.

variations

warm sweet potato salad

see base recipe page 96

warm sweet potato salad with basil & pumpkin seeds

Prepare the basic recipe, using a large handful of fresh basil in place of the coriander. Omit the macadamia nuts and sprinkle the salad with 2 tablespoons pumpkin seeds before serving.

warm sweet potato salad with mint & pine nuts

Prepare the basic recipe, replacing the coriander with 2 tablespoons chopped fresh mint. Omit the macadamia nuts and sprinkle the salad with 2 tablespoons toasted pine nuts before serving.

warm sweet potato & baby spinach salad

Prepare the basic recipe, tossing 2 large handfuls baby spinach leaves into the salad.

warm sweet potato & roast pepper salad

Prepare the basic recipe, tossing 4 roasted peppers (from a jar), sliced, into the salad.

warm sweet potato & beetroot salad

Prepare the basic recipe. Cut 200 g (7 oz) cooked beetroot (not in vinegar) into bite-sized chunks and toss into the salad.

variations

aubergine salad with pomegranate seeds, herbs & feta

see base recipe page 98

courgette salad with feta & pomegranate
Prepare the basic recipe, using 4 small–medium courgettes in place of the aubergine. (There is no need to salt the courgettes before cooking; simply slice, brush with oil and grill.)

aubergine, feta & basil salad
Prepare the basic recipe, omitting the pomegranate seeds. Toss a handful of torn fresh basil leaves with the aubergine in place of the parsley and mint sprigs.

aubergine, herb & pomegranate salad
Prepare the basic recipe, omitting the feta cheese. Replace the parsley and mint springs with 2 tablespoons chopped fresh coriander, 2 tablespoons chopped fresh flat-leaf parsley and 1 tablespoon chopped fresh mint.

aubergine, feta & sun-dried tomato salad
Prepare the basic recipe, omitting the pomegranate seeds. Instead, scatter 8 sun-dried tomatoes, drained and snipped into small bite-sized pieces, over the salad with the feta cheese.

variations

marinated vegetable carpaccio

see base recipe page 100

marinated courgettes & sweet pepper salad

Prepare the basic recipe, using 2 deseeded, thinly sliced red peppers in place of the carrots.

marinated courgettes & tomato salad

Prepare the basic recipe, omitting the carrots. Add 275 g (10 oz) halved cherry tomatoes to the sautéed courgettes before adding the marinade.

marinated vegetable carpaccio with anchovies

Prepare the basic recipe, adding 4 anchovy fillets, which have been sliced into long strips, to the sautéed vegetables before adding the marinade.

marinated vegetable carpaccio with toasted hazelnuts

Prepare the basic recipe, sprinkling the salad with 3 tablespoons chopped toasted hazelnuts just before serving.

marinated vegetable carpaccio with fresh basil

Prepare the basic recipe, using 1 bunch of torn fresh basil leaves in place of the mint.

variations

marinated leek salad

see base recipe page 102

marinated leek & sweet pepper salad
Prepare the basic recipe, sautéing 2 deseeded red peppers, cut into large chunks, with the leeks.

marinated leek salad with golden raisins
Prepare the basic recipe, adding 3 tablespoons golden raisins to the leeks with the marinade.

leek salad with mixed herb marinade
Prepare the basic recipe, using 2 tablespoons freshly chopped flat-leaf parsley, 1 tablespoon chopped fresh dill and 1 tablespoon chopped fresh mint in place of the coriander.

marinated leek & cherry tomato salad
Prepare the basic recipe, adding 225 g (8 oz) halved cherry tomatoes to the leeks with the marinade.

variations

rocket salad with sliced duck breast

see base recipe page 104

herb salad with sliced duck breast
Prepare the basic recipe, replacing the rocket with mixed salad leaves tossed with a small handful each of fresh basil and coriander leaves.

rocket salad with duck & pomegranate
Prepare the basic recipe, scattering the seeds from half a pomegranate over the salad just before serving.

rocket salad with duck & blueberries
Prepare the basic recipe, scattering 225 g (8 oz) fresh blueberries over the salad just before serving.

rocket salad with chicken
Prepare the basic recipe, using 2 boneless, skinless chicken breasts in place of the duck. Do not pan-fry, but instead bake the marinated chicken at 220°C (425°F/Gas mark 7) until just cooked through.

variations

warm duck salad with honey–orange dressing

see base recipe page 106

warm duck & peach salad
Prepare the basic recipe, replacing the mangoes with 3 peeled, pitted peaches cut into bite-sized wedges.

warm duck & kiwi salad
Prepare the basic recipe, replacing the mangoes with 3 peeled kiwi fruit, sliced into bite-sized chunks.

warm duck salad with artichoke hearts
Prepare the basic recipe, replacing the mangoes with 6 marinated artichoke hearts, cut into bite-sized wedges.

warm duck & pear salad
Prepare the basic recipe, replacing the mangoes with 3 peeled, cored pears, cut into bite-sized wedges.

variations

warm potato & egg salad

see base recipe page 108

potato, egg & spring onion salad
Prepare the basic salad, using 6 sliced spring onions in place of the shallot.

potato & chopped egg salad with capers
Prepare the basic recipe, adding 2 tablespoons roughly chopped capers to the mayonnaise mixture.

potato & quail's egg salad
Prepare the basic recipe, using 12 whole hard-boiled quail's eggs in place of the chopped hard-boiled eggs.

chopped egg & sweet potato salad
Prepare the basic recipe, using sweet potatoes in place of regular potatoes.

grain & bean salads

Whole grains, beans and lentils make a great base for salads – providing a healthy source of slow-release carbs for sustained energy, vegetarian protein and essential fibre. They're wholesome, flavourful and incredibly versatile – just perfect for making into exciting salad combinations.

coriander tabbouleh

see variations page 137

A Middle Eastern classic made with nutty bulgur wheat, lemony tabbouleh makes a wonderful accompaniment, particularly for grilled meats and fish.

275 ml (10 fl. oz) vegetable stock
175 g (6 oz) bulgur wheat
1 red onion, halved and thinly sliced
1 bunch fresh flat-leaf parsley, roughly chopped
1 bunch fresh coriander, roughly chopped
700 g (1½ lb) diced, deseeded tomatoes
3 tbsp lemon juice
4 tbsp olive oil
salt and freshly ground pepper

Heat the stock in a saucepan, stir in the bulgur wheat, turn off the burner and leave to stand for 30 minutes. Then fluff up with a fork and leave to cool.

Mix the sliced onion, chopped herbs and diced tomatoes with the lemon juice, olive oil, salt and pepper. Then combine with the bulgur wheat. Season to taste and leave to stand for 20 minutes. Season again with salt and pepper before serving.

Serves 4

quinoa with rosemary & peppers

see variations page 138

Highly nutritious and one of the only grains that constitute a whole protein, quinoa has been eaten for thousands of years. It was cultivated by the ancient Incas.

400 g (14 oz) quinoa
2 red peppers, diced
1 x 400-g (14-oz) tin corn kernels, drained
2 spring onions, sliced in thin rings
juice of 1/2 lemon
1 tsp honey
3 tbsp grapeseed oil (or canola oil)
2 tbsp wine vinegar
2 tbsp chopped fresh rosemary
1/2 tsp dried coriander
1/2 tsp fennel seeds
salt and freshly ground pepper

Cook the quinoa in salted water over low heat for about 15 minutes. Drain. Toss the quinoa with the diced pepper, sweet corn, spring onion rings, lemon juice, honey, oil, vinegar, rosemary, coriander and fennel seeds.

Taste, season with salt and pepper as needed. Chill for 30 minutes and check the seasoning before serving.

Serves 4

warm chickpea salad with aubergine & courgette

see variations page 139

This wholesome, nutritious salad makes a great vegetarian lunch or supper, but it is also fabulous with grilled meat or fish.

3 tbsp canola or olive oil
1 small–medium aubergine, diced
2 small–medium courgettes, sliced
1 tsp fennel seeds
75–100 ml (3–4 fl. oz) vegetable stock
4 tbsp soy sauce
1 x 400-g (14-oz) tin chickpeas, washed and drained
50–100 g (2–4 oz) pitted black olives
cayenne pepper
2 handfuls cress

In a large frying pan, heat the oil. Add the aubergine, courgettes and fennel seeds, and sauté. Add the vegetable stock and soy sauce and cook for about 4 minutes. Stir in the chickpeas and olives and season to taste with cayenne pepper. Serve on a bed of cress.

Serves 4

rice salad with mozzarella & peppers

see variations page 140

When grilled, peppers become deliciously sweet, adding a luscious, juicy punch of taste and colour to this simple rice salad.

175 g (6 oz) rice
1 red pepper
1 yellow pepper
1 orange pepper
3 tbsp olive oil, plus extra for drizzling
salt and freshly ground pepper
50 g (2 oz) pitted black olives
300 g (11 oz) mini-mozzarellas
1 bunch rocket, separated
3 tbsp white balsamic vinegar
fresh basil leaves, to garnish

Steam the rice according to the packet instructions. When done, remove from heat and leave to cool.

Wash and halve the peppers, remove the seeds and the white inner ribs and roughly dice the flesh. Put on a baking tray lined with waxed paper and drizzle with olive oil. Season with salt and pepper and put under a preheated grill for about 4 minutes. Remove and leave to cool.

Put the cooked rice, peppers, olives, mozzarellas and rocket into a serving bowl. Mix with 3 tablespoons oil and the balsamic vinegar. Season to taste with salt and pepper and garnish with fresh basil before serving.

Serves 4

green bean & chickpea salad with cherry tomatoes & red onion

see variations page 141

This brightly coloured salad is packed with healthy, nutritious ingredients and makes a great vegetarian lunch or supper, but is also good served as an accompaniment at a barbecue.

700 g (1½ lb) green beans
175 g (6 oz) chickpeas, drained and rinsed
225 g (8 oz) halved cherry tomatoes

for the dressing:
3 tbsp white wine vinegar
4 tbsp olive oil
salt and freshly ground pepper
3 tbsp finely chopped fresh basil
1 red onion, diced

Wash, trim and halve the green beans and cook in boiling, salted water until tender, about 6–10 minutes. Drain, refresh in cold water and drain well. Put the beans, chickpeas and tomatoes in a serving bowl.

To make the dressing, mix the vinegar with the olive oil, salt and pepper. Stir in the basil and onion and check the seasoning. Mix with the beans, chickpeas and tomatoes, and leave to stand for a while before serving.

Serves 2

lenticchie all'umbra

see variations page 142

This simple rustic salad of lentils with tomatoes and pancetta has a wonderfully rich, earthy flavour and makes a great accompaniment to summer meals.

- 2 tbsp olive oil
- 175 g (6 oz) finely diced pancetta
- 2 cloves garlic, finely chopped
- 2–3 sprigs of fresh thyme, leaves removed
- 2–3 sprigs of fresh sage, leaves removed and shredded
- 450 g (1 lb) brown or greenish lentils (preferably small)
- about 450 ml (16 fl. oz) mixed red wine and stock (or just stock)
- 700 g (1½ lb) peeled, deseeded and diced tomatoes
- salt and freshly ground pepper
- white wine vinegar, to taste
- fresh basil leaves, to garnish

Heat the oil in a deep frying pan and fry the pancetta until crisp. Remove about a third of the pancetta and set aside. Add the garlic, herbs and lentils to the frying pan and sauté briefly. Add the mixed red wine and stock, cover and cook over moderate heat for 40–50 minutes until the lentils are almost soft.

Add the diced tomatoes to the pan, mix and cook for another 10 minutes or so. Season with salt and pepper and add a little vinegar to taste. Serve sprinkled with the basil and the reserved pancetta.

Serves 4

wild rice salad with walnuts & dried cranberries

see variations page 143

Wild rice has long, slim grains and a nuttier, firmer texture than regular rice. This salad, with its nuts, dried cranberries, herbs and spicy dressing, makes a great side dish.

225 g (8 oz) wild rice
175 g (6 oz) chopped walnuts
2 tbsp chopped fresh mint
50 g (2 oz) dried cranberries
juice of 1 lemon
2 tbsp peanut oil (or canola oil)
salt and cayenne pepper

Cook the rice in boiling, salted water for about 40 minutes, or until done. Drain and leave to cool. Mix the rice with the rest of the ingredients and season to taste with salt and cayenne pepper.

Serves 4

green bean salad with sesame & coriander

see variations page 144

Fresh, sweet green beans are one of the joys of summer. Try this simple green bean salad spiked with Asian flavours at your next alfresco meal.

550–700 g (1¼–1½ lb) green beans
1 tbsp butter
1 clove garlic, finely chopped
1-cm (½-in) piece of fresh root ginger, peeled and finely diced
2 tbsp peanut oil (or canola oil)
3–4 tbsp dark soy sauce
1–2 tbsp rice vinegar
2 tbsp sesame seeds
salt and pepper
pinch of sugar
1 tsp finely chopped coriander, to serve

Wash, top and tail the beans, and halve if necessary. Blanch in plenty of boiling, salted water until tender, about 6–10 minutes. Drain and refresh in ice-cold water.

Heat the butter in a frying pan, add the garlic and ginger and sauté, stirring. Add the peanut oil and the beans. Stir in the soy sauce, rice vinegar and sesame seeds. Season with salt, pepper and a pinch of sugar. Sprinkle with coriander. Serve in bowls, warm or cold.

Serves 4

bean salad with red onions & parsley

see variations page 145

A simple bean salad makes a great addition to a barbecue or buffet, but is also a delicious accompaniment to serve with kebabs and other grilled meats.

225 g (8 oz) dried flageolet beans
2 tbsp oil
2 red onions, finely chopped
1 bay leaf
175 ml (6 fl. oz) vegetable stock
3 tbsp white wine vinegar or to taste
salt and freshly ground pepper
1 bunch fresh parsley, chopped

Soak the beans in water, to cover, overnight. In the morning, drain, rinse and drain again.

In a large saucepan, heat the oil and sauté the onions. Add the beans and bay leaf and stir in the stock. The beans must be covered by the stock; add more stock as needed. Cover and simmer for about 15 minutes or until tender, then remove from the heat. Season with salt and pepper, add vinegar to taste and leave to cool. Then remove the bay leaf and mix in the parsley. Check the seasoning and serve.

Serves 4

variations

coriander tabbouleh

see base recipe page 121

coriander tabbouleh with smoked trout
Prepare the basic recipe, adding 2 flaked smoked trout fillets with the chopped herbs and tomatoes.

coriander tabbouleh with poached eggs
Prepare the basic recipe. To serve, poach 4 eggs in boiling water for about 4 minutes, then lift out and pat dry on paper towels. Spoon the tabbouleh into 4 bowls and top each serving with a poached egg.

coriander tabbouleh with ham
Prepare the basic recipe, adding 200 g (7 oz) ham cut into strips with the chopped herbs and tomatoes.

coriander tabbouleh with chickpeas
Prepare the basic recipe, adding 400 g (14 oz) tinned chickpeas (drained and rinsed) with the chopped herbs and tomatoes.

classic mint tabbouleh
Prepare the basic recipe, replacing the coriander with 1 small bunch of chopped, fresh mint.

variations

quinoa with rosemary & peppers

see base recipe page 122

bulgur wheat with rosemary & peppers
Prepare the basic recipe, using bulgur wheat in place of the quinoa. Instead of boiling, simply put the bulgur in a bowl, cover with boiling water and leave to stand for 20 minutes before draining.

quinoa with rosemary, peppers & halloumi
Prepare the basic recipe. Cut 225 g (8 oz) halloumi into 5-mm (1/4-inch) thick slices, then grill on both sides until golden. Toss into the salad.

couscous with rosemary & peppers
Prepare the basic recipe, using couscous in place of the quinoa. Instead of boiling, put the couscous in a bowl, mix in 1 tablespoon olive oil and a pinch of salt, then pour in 600 ml (1 pint) boiling water and leave to stand for 5 minutes. Fluff up the grains before tossing with the other ingredients.

quinoa with rosemary, peppers & borlotti beans
Prepare the basic recipe, adding 2 x 400-g (14-oz) tins borlotti beans, drained.

quinoa with sage & red peppers
Prepare the basic recipe, using 1/2 tablespoon chopped fresh sage in place of the rosemary.

variations

warm chickpea salad with aubergine & courgette

see base recipe page 124

warm flageolet bean salad with aubergine & courgette
Prepare the basic recipe, using flageolet beans in place of the chickpeas.

warm chickpea salad with courgette & sweet peppers
Prepare the basic recipe, replacing the aubergine with 2 deseeded red or yellow peppers cut into large strips.

warm chickpea salad with aubergine, courgette & spinach
Prepare the basic recipe, using 4 handfuls of baby spinach leaves in place of the cress.

warm chickpea & tomato salad with aubergine & courgette
Prepare the basic recipe, adding 275 g (10 oz) cherry tomatoes with the chickpeas and olives.

warm chickpea & caraway salad with aubergine & courgette
Prepare the basic recipe, replacing the fennel seeds with 1 teaspoon caraway seeds.

variations

rice salad with mozzarella & peppers

see base recipe page 126

rice salad with feta & peppers
Prepare the basic recipe, replacing the mozzarella with 225 g (8 oz) roughly crumbled feta cheese.

rice salad with stilton & peppers
Prepare the basic recipe, replacing the mozzarella with 225 g (8 oz) cubed Stilton cheese.

rice salad with mozzarella, peppers & pistachios
Prepare the basic recipe, adding 4 tablespoons roughly chopped pistachio nuts with the grilled peppers and olives.

rice salad with mozzarella, peppers & pine nuts
Prepare the basic recipe, adding 4 tablespoons toasted pine nuts with the grilled peppers and olives.

variations

green bean & chickpea salad with cherry tomatoes & red onion

see base recipe page 128

three-bean salad with red onion
Prepare the basic recipe, omitting the chickpeas and tomatoes, and adding 100 g (4 oz) canned, rinsed butter beans and 100 g (4 oz) canned, rinsed flageolet beans.

green bean & chickpea salad with lemon dressing
Prepare the basic recipe, adding 1 teaspoon finely grated lemon zest to the dressing.

chickpea salad with mangetout, cherry tomatoes & red onion
Prepare the basic recipe, using mangetout in place of the green beans. Cook them for 2 minutes only, then refresh in cold water.

green bean & chickpea salad with thyme dressing
Prepare the basic recipe, replacing the basil with 1 teaspoon fresh thyme leaves.

borlotti & green bean salad with cherry tomatoes & red onion
Prepare the basic recipe, using drained, rinsed tinned borlotti beans in place of the chickpeas.

variations

lenticchie all'umbra

see base recipe page 130

lentil & bacon salad with sweet peppers
Prepare the basic recipe, using 8 strips bacon, snipped into small pieces, in place of the pancetta. Replace the tomatoes with 2 deseeded and diced red or yellow peppers.

lentil & pancetta salad with fresh herbs
Prepare the basic recipe, adding a small handful of fresh coriander leaves and 2 tablespoons snipped fresh chives to the frying pan with the tomatoes.

lentil, tomato & pancetta salad with sweet peas
Prepare the basic recipe. Cook 225 g (8 oz) frozen peas in boiling water for about 3 minutes, then drain, refresh under cold water, and toss into the salad before garnishing with basil.

spicy lentil & tomato salad
Prepare the basic recipe, adding 1/4 teaspoon crushed dried chilli flakes with the garlic and herbs.

variations

wild rice salad with walnuts & dried cranberries

see base recipe page 132

wild rice salad with pistachios & dates
Prepare the basic recipe, using 6 tablespoons pistachios and 8 chopped dates in place of the walnuts and cranberries.

wild rice salad with avocado, walnuts & dried cranberries
Prepare the basic recipe, adding 2 pitted, peeled and diced avocados with the walnuts and cranberries.

wild rice salad with watercress, walnuts & dried cranberries
Prepare the basic recipe, adding a large handful of roughly chopped watercress with the walnuts and cranberries.

wild rice salad with fresh herbs, walnuts & dried cranberries
Prepare the basic recipe, adding a handful of roughly chopped fresh parsley, 1 teaspoon fresh thyme leaves and 1 tablespoon chopped fresh chives.

wild rice salad with apple, celery & walnuts
Prepare the basic recipe, using 1 cored, diced apple and 2 sliced celery stalks in place of the cranberries.

variations

green bean salad with sesame & coriander

see base recipe page 134

green bean salad with sesame, coriander & chilli
Prepare the basic recipe, adding ½ finely chopped deseeded red chilli pepper with the garlic and ginger.

fava bean salad with sesame & coriander
Prepare the basic recipe, using shelled fava beans in place of the green beans. Blanch them for 3–6 minutes until just tender.

courgette salad with sesame & coriander
Prepare the basic recipe, using 3 thickly sliced courgettes in place of the green beans and blanch for several minutes until just tender.

green bean & carrot salad with sesame & coriander
Prepare the basic recipe, replacing half the green beans with 4 carrots, cut into sticks. Blanch the carrots for 3 minutes, then refresh under cold water.

green bean salad with coriander & peanuts
Prepare the basic recipe, using 3 tablespoons roughly chopped peanuts in place of the sesame seeds.

variations

bean salad with red onions & parsley

see base recipe page 136

flageobean & red onion salad with balsamic dressing
Prepare the basic recipe, using 2 tablespoons balsamic vinegar in place of the wine vinegar.

flageolet bean & red onion salad with chives
Prepare the basic recipe, adding 2 tablespoons snipped fresh chives with the parsley.

butter bean & red onion salad
Prepare the basic recipe, using butter beans in place of the flageolet beans.

cannellini bean & red onion salad
Prepare the basic recipe, using cannellini beans in place of the flageolet beans.

flageolet bean, red onion & tuna salad
Prepare the basic salad, stirring 2–2½ x 185-g (6½-oz) tins drained, flaked tuna into the salad with the parsley.

pasta salads

Popular with kids and adults alike, pasta salads are loved by everyone. Whether you choose plain, flavoured, wholemeal or stuffed pasta to make your salad – it will provide a healthy, sustaining source of energy for you and your family.

orzo salad with vegetables & feta

see variations page 163

Orzo is a tiny rice-shaped pasta that's particularly popular in Greece. It's great for salads, and this tangy recipe makes an easy lunchbox meal.

450 g (1 lb) orzo
450 g (1 lb) fresh asparagus
2 tbsp pine nuts
3 tbsp olive oil
12 cherry peppers, halved
2 yellow peppers, diced
juice and zest of 1/2 lemon
salt and freshly ground pepper
175 g (6 oz) feta cheese
fresh basil leaves, to garnish

Cook the orzo in plenty of boiling, salted water according to the packet instructions, until al dente. Drain, refresh in cold water and drain well. Wash the asparagus and cut at an angle into approximately 2.5-cm (1-inch) lengths. Toast the pine nuts in a dry frying pan until golden brown. Leave to cool.

Heat the oil in a frying pan and sauté the peppers and asparagus for about 2 minutes, stirring. Add the lemon zest and orzo and warm through. Add salt, pepper and lemon juice to taste.

Spoon onto plates. Scatter with crumbled feta, sprinkle with the toasted pine nuts and garnish with basil.

Serves 4

x14

colourful fusilli salad

see variations page 164

Using pasta shapes coloured with spinach and tomato can create a stunning salad that's just too appealing to resist.

225 g (8 oz) tricolour fusilli
175 g (6 oz) green beans
1 celery stalk, sliced
1 red pepper, diced
generous 50 g (2 oz) pitted and sliced black olives
4 tbsp olive oil
4 tbsp white wine vinegar
salt and freshly ground pepper
cayenne pepper
8 lettuce leaves, such as butterhead, to serve

Cook the fusilli in boiling salted water according to the packet instructions, until al dente, then drain.

Trim the green beans and blanch in salted water for about 4 minutes, then place immediately in cold water to halt the cooking process. Drain, then cut the beans in half. Blanch the celery for about 2 minutes.

Mix the olive oil, vinegar, salt, pepper and cayenne pepper together in a large bowl. Add the pasta, beans, celery, red pepper and olives. Taste and add more salt, pepper and cayenne if desired. Leave to marinate for about 15 minutes. Place 2 lettuce leaves on each plate, top with a serving of the salad and serve.

Serves 4

couscous salad

see variations page 165

Although most people think of it as a grain, light, fluffy couscous is actually a type of pasta. It is fabulous for simple salads because it is able to carry the flavour of other ingredients brilliantly.

about 700 ml (1¼ pint) vegetable stock
700 g (1½ lb) couscous
50 g (2 oz) raisins
50 g (2 oz) currants
1 red pepper, diced
1 green pepper, diced
50 g (2 oz) sun-dried tomatoes in oil, roughly chopped
1 onion, diced
2 tbsp white wine vinegar
2 tbsp lemon juice
3 tbsp olive oil
salt and freshly ground pepper
½ small bunch fresh mint, roughly chopped

Bring the vegetable stock to the boil. Put the couscous, raisins and currants into a bowl. Pour the boiling stock into the bowl. Leave the couscous to stand for about 10 minutes, then fluff with a fork.

Put the diced peppers, tomatoes and onion in a serving bowl. Whisk together the vinegar, lemon juice and olive oil to make a dressing. Season with salt and pepper, and pour it over the vegetables. Add the couscous and mint, toss to combine and serve.

Serves 4

orecchiette with beans & rocket pesto

see variations page 166

In Italy, the word orecchiette means 'little ears', which perfectly describes these domed pasta shapes. They require slightly longer cooking than regular pasta and have a deliciously chewy texture.

225 g (8 oz) canned kidney beans in water
about 1 tbsp olive oil
1 clove garlic, finely chopped
75–100 ml (3–4 fl. oz) white wine
75–100 ml (3–4 fl. oz) vegetable stock
450 g (1 lb) orecchiette
450 g (1 lb) roughly chopped fresh spinach

for the pesto
1 bunch fresh rocket, roughly chopped and tough stems removed
2 tbsp pine nuts
1 tbsp freshly grated Parmesan
1 clove garlic
about 6 tbsp olive oil
sea salt and freshly ground pepper

Drain the beans and rinse gently. In a saucepan, heat the olive oil and briefly sauté the garlic. Add the drained beans, then stir in the white wine and stock. Boil vigorously for 10 minutes, then turn down and simmer for 10 minutes. Drain and transfer to a large salad bowl.

Cook the orecchiette according to the package instructions until al dente. Drain and add to the kidney beans.

To make the pesto, put the rocket, pine nuts, Parmesan, garlic and a little olive oil in a

food processor or blender. Process, adding more olive oil in a thin stream, until the pesto is smooth and creamy. Season to taste with salt and pepper.

Add the spinach to the beans and pasta. Then add the pesto and toss to combine. Season to taste before serving.

Serves 4

pasta salad with ham & peas

see variations page 167

Ham and peas are a classic combination – whether in soup, risotto or as here in this chunky pasta salad. Kids will love it, but so will the grownups.

275 g (10 oz) frozen peas
1 large carrot
2 spring onions
350 g (12 oz) caserecce or macaroni
400 g (14 oz) kassler (smoked and cured pork loin) or turkey ham
100 g (4 oz) cheddar, grated

for the dressing:
4 tbsp mayonnaise
scant 100 ml (4 fl. oz) sour cream
175–225 ml (6–8 fl. oz) cream
pinch of paprika
salt and pepper

Thaw the peas. Peel the carrot and cut into julienne strips. Trim the spring onions and cut at an angle into approximately 5-mm (1/4-inch) rings.

Cook the pasta in plenty of boiling, salted water according to the packet instructions, adding the peas, carrots and spring onions after 5 minutes. Continue cooking until the pasta is al dente. Drain in a colander, then refresh in cold water, drain well and leave to cool.

Cut the pork (or turkey ham) into approximately 1-cm (1/2-inch) cubes. Add the cheese and ham to the cooled pasta and vegetables, mix and season well with a pinch of paprika, salt and pepper.

To make the dressing, mix all the ingredients together. Taste and adjust the seasoning. Pour the dressing over the salad, mix well and season again. Serve on plates with a garnish of your choice.

Serves 4

farfalle with prawns & artichokes

see variations page 168

Combining prawns and artichoke in this simple recipe creates a sophisticated salad that's great for alfresco entertaining or a no-fuss lunch with friends.

350 g (12 oz) farfalle
350 g (12 oz) mini-artichokes
juice of 1 lemon
2 ripe tomatoes, quartered, seeds removed
icing sugar, for sprinkling
12 raw prawns, peeled (apart from tail) and deveined
100 g (4 oz) bacon slices, cut in thin strips
1 clove garlic, finely chopped
olive oil, for drizzling
3 tbsp white wine vinegar
sea salt and freshly ground pepper
freshly grated Parmesan, to serve

Cook the farfalle in boiling salted water according to packet instructions until al dente. Drain. Clean and quarter the artichokes. Place in cold water with half the lemon juice.

Place the tomatoes on a baking pan lined with parchment paper. Sprinkle with icing sugar. Add the prawns, drained artichokes, bacon and garlic to the pan. Drizzle olive oil over everything and sprinkle with salt and pepper. Place under a preheated grill for about 2 minutes. Turn all ingredients over and grill for a further 2 minutes.

Put the farfalle in a large serving bowl. Add the tomatoes, prawns, artichokes, bacon and garlic. Drizzle olive oil over the top and mix in the vinegar and remaining lemon juice. Season with salt and pepper and serve with grated Parmesan.

Serves 4

pasta salad with prawns

see variations page 169

You can toss this very easy salad together in no time, making it the perfect choice for a midweek supper.

350 g (12 oz) penne
3 tbsp ricotta cheese
3 tbsp white balsamic vinegar
2 tbsp olive oil
225 g (8 oz) cooked prawns
1 bunch fresh coriander, finely chopped
salt and freshly ground pepper
2 tbsp freshly grated Parmesan

Cook the penne in boiling salted water according to packet instructions until al dente. Drain and cool.

In a serving bowl, mix together the ricotta cheese, balsamic vinegar and olive oil. Stir until smooth. Add the drained pasta, prawns and coriander, and toss to combine. Season to taste with salt and pepper and sprinkle with the Parmesan before serving.

Serves 4

pasta alla villana

see variations page 170

There are many different types of spiral-shaped pasta such as fusilli, radiatore and rotini. Any will be delicious in this recipe. This pasta salad can be served warm or cold.

450 g (1 lb) spiral pasta
300 g (11 oz) fresh asparagus
2 tbsp oil
100 g (4 oz) sliced, smoked ham, cut in thin strips
2 chopped garlic cloves
175–225 ml (6–8 fl. oz) vegetable stock
175 g (6 oz) pitted black olives
100 g (4 oz) sun-dried tomatoes in oil, chopped
2 tbsp chopped fresh marjoram
2 tbsp chopped fresh thyme
salt and freshly ground pepper
fresh marjoram, to garnish

Cook the pasta in boiling, salted water according to the packet instructions. While it is cooking, peel the lower third of each asparagus spear and cut the spears into approximately 2.5-cm (1-in) lengths.

Heat the oil in a large saucepan. Sauté the ham, garlic and asparagus. Add the stock, cover and cook for about 5 minutes. Then add the olives, tomatoes, herbs and drained pasta. Toss to combine. Season to taste with salt and pepper.

Serve warm or cold, garnished with marjoram.

Serves 4

greek tortellini salad

see variations page 171

Tortellini are available with a huge variety of fillings – although traditionally they are stuffed with chopped meat or cheese. For this recipe, choose one that will go well with courgettes and sheep's cheese, such as spinach and ricotta, sun-dried tomato or wild mushroom.

2 small–medium courgettes
6 tbsp olive oil
2 small red peppers, diced
1 tbp finely grated lemon zest
juice of 1 lemon
1 tbp fresh thyme leaves
1 tbp chopped fresh rosemary leaves
1 tbsp chopped fresh parsley
salt and freshly ground pepper
400 g (14 oz) tortellini
200 g (7 oz) crumbled feta, to garnish
100 g (4 oz) sliced black olives, to garnish

Wash the courgettes, quarter lengthways and cut into bite-sized pieces. Heat 2 tablespoons of the olive oil in a frying pan and sauté the diced peppers and courgettes for 3–4 minutes. Remove and leave to cool.

Mix the remaining 4 tablespoons oil with the lemon zest and juice, herbs, salt and pepper to make a dressing. Mix with the sautéed vegetables and leave to stand.

Meanwhile, cook the tortellini according to the packet instructions. Drain and add to the vegetables. Mix and season to taste. Serve garnished with the feta and olives. Serve warm or room temperature.

Serves 4

variations

orzo salad with vegetables & feta

see base recipe page 147

fusilli salad with vegetables and feta
Prepare the basic recipe, using fusilli in place of the orzo.

orzo salad with peppers, courgettes & feta
Prepare the basic recipe, using 2 sliced courgettes in place of the asparagus.

orzo salad with vegetables & goat's cheese
Prepare the basic recipe, using diced goat's cheese in place of the feta.

orzo salad with pepper, peas & feta
Prepare the basic recipe, using 225 g (8 oz) frozen peas in place of the asparagus. Cook peas in boiling water for 2 minutes, then drain and toss with the sautéed peppers and orzo.

orzo salad with vegetables, feta & mint
Prepare the basic recipe, omitting the basil leaves. Instead, toss 1½ tablespoons chopped fresh mint with the orzo and sautéed vegetables.

variations

colourful fusilli pasta salad

see base recipe page 148

colourful fusilli salad with kidney beans
Prepare the basic recipe, adding 1 x 400-g (14-oz) tin drained, rinsed kidney beans with the drained pasta and vegetables.

colourful fusilli salad with vegetables & capers
Prepare the basic recipe, adding 1½ tablespoons roughly chopped capers to the drained pasta and vegetables.

colourful fusilli salad with red-hot chilli peppers
Prepare the basic recipe, omitting the cayenne pepper. Instead, add 2 chopped, bottled peppadew peppers to the drained pasta and vegetables.

colourful fusilli salad with fresh herbs
Prepare the basic recipe, adding 3 tablespoons chopped fresh flat leaf parsley, a small handful of torn fresh basil leaves, and 2 tablespoons snipped fresh chives.

variations

couscous salad

see base recipe page 150

couscous salad with cranberries & walnuts

Prepare the basic recipe, using 100 g (4 oz) dried cranberries in place of the currants and raisins. Add a handful of walnut pieces to the peppers and tomatoes.

couscous salad with toasted pine nuts

Prepare the basic recipe, adding 4 tablespoons toasted pine nuts with the peppers and tomatoes.

couscous salad with goat's cheese

Prepare the basic recipe, scattering 225 g (8 oz) diced goat's cheese over the salad.

couscous salad with fresh apple

Prepare the basic recipe, omitting the currants. Add 2 cored, diced apples to the peppers and tomatoes.

couscous salad with spring onions

Prepare the basic recipe, omitting the onion and adding 5 sliced spring onions to the peppers and tomatoes.

variations

orecchiette with beans & rocket pesto

see base recipe page 152

orecchiette with beans & fresh basil pesto
Prepare the basic recipe, using 2 small bunches fresh basil in place of the rocket.

orecchiette with beans, tomato & spinach
Prepare the basic recipe, adding 275 g (10 oz) halved cherry tomatoes with the spinach.

orecchiette & bean salad with cheat's pesto dressing
Prepare the basic recipe, omitting the rocket pesto. Instead, stir 2 tablespoons olive oil into 3 tablespoons ready-made pesto, drizzle over the salad and toss.

orecchiette & bean salad with simple mustard dressing
Prepare the basic recipe, omitting the rocket pesto. Instead, whisk together 2 tablespoons balsamic vinegar with 3 tablespoons olive oil and 1½ teaspoons whole-grain mustard. Drizzle it over the salad and toss to combine.

orecchiette & bean salad with anchovies
Prepare the basic recipe, adding 8 anchovy fillets, sliced lengthways, to the drained beans, pasta and spinach.

variations

pasta salad with ham & peas

see base recipe page 154

pasta salad with smoked trout & peas
Prepare the basic recipe, omitting the ham and cheese. Instead, add 3 flaked smoked trout fillets.

pasta salad with ham, peas & blue cheese
Prepare the basic recipe, using 175 g (6 oz) crumbled blue cheese in place of the cheddar.

pasta salad with ham, peas & celery
Prepare the basic recipe, adding 3 stalks of celery, sliced, with the peas and carrot.

pasta salad with ham, apple & celery
Prepare the basic recipe, omitting the peas. Instead, add 2 stalks sliced celery and 2 cored, diced apples.

pasta salad with ham, peas & rocket
Prepare the basic recipe. Place a large handful of rocket leaves on each plate and pile the salad on top.

variations

farfalle with prawns & artichokes

see base recipe page 156

farfalle with crab & artichokes
Prepare the basic recipe, omitting the prawns. Instead, add 2 small tins white crabmeat (drained) to the pasta, artichokes, tomato and bacon.

penne with prawns & artichokes
Prepare the basic recipe, using penne in place of the farfalle.

spicy farfalle with prawns & artichokes
Prepare the basic recipe, sprinkling $\frac{1}{4}$–$\frac{1}{2}$ teaspoon crushed dried chilli pepper over the tomatoes, artichokes and prawns before grilling.

farfalle with prawns, artichokes & chives
Prepare the basic recipe, sprinkling 2 tablespoons snipped fresh chives over the salad before tossing.

farfalle with chicken & artichokes
Prepare the basic recipe, omitting the prawns. Instead, grill 3 boneless, skinless chicken breasts. Slice them and add to the farfalle, tomatoes and artichokes before tossing.

pasta salad with prawns

see base recipe page 158

pasta salad with prawns & sun-dried tomatoes
Prepare the basic recipe, adding 8 sun-dried tomatoes, drained and snipped into bite-sized pieces with the prawns.

pasta salad with prawns & mangetout
Prepare the basic recipe. While the pasta cooks, blanch 225 g (8 oz) mangetout for about 2 minutes, then drain and refresh under cold water before tossing with the pasta and prawns.

pasta salad with lemon–ricotta dressing
Prepare the basic recipe, whisking 1 teaspoon finely grated lemon zest into the dressing.

pasta salad with ham & ricotta dressing
Prepare the basic recipe, using 225 g (8 oz) diced ham in place of the prawns.

pasta salad with prawns & dill
Prepare the basic recipe, using 3 tablespoons snipped fresh dill in place of the coriander.

variations

pasta alla villana

see base recipe page 160

garganelli salad with ham & asparagus
Prepare the basic recipe, using garganelli pasta in place of the spirals.

pasta salad with smoked salmon & asparagus
Prepare the basic recipe, omitting the ham. Instead, add 100 g (4 oz) smoked salmon, cut into strips, with the olives, tomatoes and herbs.

pasta salad with spring vegetables & ham
Prepare the basic recipe, using 150 g (5 oz) asparagus, 175 g (6 oz) frozen peas, and 175 g (6 oz) shelled broad beans. Add the peas and beans to the pan with the stock and cook until they are tender.

pasta salad with asparagus, ham & roasted peppers
Prepare the basic recipe, using a jar (about 250 g/9 oz) roasted red peppers (drained, but not chopped) in place of the sun-dried tomatoes.

pasta salad with courgette & ham
Prepare the basic recipe, using 3 sliced courgettes in place of the asparagus and reduce the cooking time to 2 minutes.

greek tortellini salad

see base recipe page 162

greek ravioli salad
Prepare the basic recipe, using ravioli in place of the tortellini.

greek-style penne salad
Prepare the basic recipe, using 350 g (12 oz) penne in place of the tortellini.

courgette & tortellini salad
Prepare the basic recipe, omitting the crumbled feta. Instead, serve the salad topped with shavings of Parmesan cheese.

greek tagliatelle salad
Prepare the basic recipe, using 350 g (12 oz) tagliatelle in place of the tortellini.

slaws & shredded salads

Crisp, crunchy vegetables and fruits such as cabbage, carrot and green papaya are perfect for shredding and turning into tasty slaws and salads. Whether you go for a classic, creamy coleslaw or a spicy Asian-style shredded salad, there are countless delicious recipes to choose from.

carrot salad with pearl onions & parsley

see variations page 185

This cooked vegetable salad with its light, tangy dressing makes a great accompaniment to grilled meats and fish. It is also a good choice for a light appetiser.

25 g (1 oz) butter
800 g (1¾ lb) carrot sticks
350 g (9 oz) pearl onions, peeled
75–100 ml (3–4 fl. oz) vegetable stock
4 cloves garlic, sliced
1 bunch fresh parsley, roughly chopped
salt and pepper
white wine vinegar

Heat the butter in a saucepan and sauté the carrot sticks and onions. Add the stock, cover, and cook over medium heat for 5 minutes. Add the sliced garlic to the pan after 2–3 minutes.

When the vegetables are cooked, but still retain a little bite, remove from the heat, mix in the parsley, and season with salt and pepper. Add vinegar to taste and leave to cool slightly. Put the carrot salad on individual plates and serve warm or cold.

Serves 4

green papaya & chilli salad

see variations page 186

This light, zesty salad is a simplified version of the classic spicy papaya eaten in Thailand. It's particularly good served with coconut rice.

1–2 green papayas (700 g/1½ lb)
2 kaffir lime leaves
2 chillies

for the dressing:
zest and juice of 1 lime
2 tbsp light fish sauce
1 tbsp brown sugar
2 cloves garlic, sliced

Peel, wash, halve, and seed the papayas. Shred finely, using a mandoline vegetable slicer if available. Finely shred the kaffir lime leaves. Halve and seed the chillies and slice very finely.

To make the dressing, mix the lime zest and juice with the fish sauce and brown sugar. Add the garlic.

Mix the shredded papaya with the dressing and pile into bowls. Sprinkle with the lime leaves and sliced chilli and serve.

Serves 4

two-tone coleslaw

see variations page 187

Crisp and crunchy coleslaw is one of those salads that's perfect for every occasion. It's great in winter when other salad vegetables are out of season, but it's a fabulous dish for barbecues and a must for any buffet table or family meal. This coleslaw is especially colourful.

225 g (8 oz) green cabbage
225 g (8 oz) red cabbage
1 carrot
1 apple

for the dressing:
2 tbsp mayonnaise
1 tbsp crème fraîche
1 tsp dry mustard
pinch sugar
2 tbsp white wine vinegar
2 tbsp raisins
salt and pepper

Wash the green cabbage and the red cabbage and remove the stems. Slice or shred into thin strips. Peel the carrot and the apple. Quarter the apple and remove the core. Grate the apple and the carrot very thinly. Put the cabbage, carrot and apple in a large serving bowl.

In a small bowl, combine the mayonnaise, crème fraîche, dry mustard, sugar, vinegar and raisins. Season with salt and pepper. Pour over the salad and toss to combine. Leave to stand for 15 minutes and season again before serving.

Serves 4

country slaw

see variations page 188

This crunchy and colourful slaw made with crisp, raw vegetables has a simple, rustic feel. Make it in late summer when sweet peppers and tender courgettes are at their best.

2 stalks celery, thinly sliced
4 carrots, peeled and cut into matchsticks
2 courgettes, cut into matchsticks
2 red peppers, cut into thin strips
1 bunch fresh basil, chopped

for the dressing:
2 tbsp white balsamic vinegar
2 tbsp lemon juice
1 tsp honey
3 tbsp grapeseed oil or canola oil
salt and freshly ground pepper
fresh basil leaves, to garnish

Put the celery, carrots, courgettes, peppers and chopped basil into a large bowl.

In a small bowl, mix the balsamic vinegar with the lemon juice, honey and oil. Pour the dressing over the vegetables and toss to combine. Season to taste with salt and pepper. Serve in individual bowls, garnished with basil.

Serves 4

red cabbage salad with jicama & peppers

see variations page 189

Jicama, native to South America, is a root vegetable with a mild, nutty flavour. It can either be cooked or used raw in salads. This salad goes very well with grilled food.

2 red peppers
2 yellow peppers
½ red cabbage
1 carrot
400 g (14 oz) jicama
3 tbsp olive oil
2 tbsp white wine vinegar
2 tbsp fresh lime juice
1 tsp honey
salt and cayenne pepper
2 tbsp fresh coriander leaves

Wash and halve the peppers, remove the seeds and the white inner ribs, and cut the flesh into very thin strips. Trim the red cabbage, remove the stalk, and shred the leaves. Peel and shred the carrot and jicama (using a mandoline vegetable slicer if available). Place all the vegetables in a large serving bowl, and toss.

Mix the olive oil, vinegar, lime juice and honey. Season to taste with salt and cayenne pepper.

Pour the dressing over the salad ingredients, combine and leave to stand for at least 1 hour. Garnish with the coriander before serving.

Serves 4

insalata trevigiana

see variations page 190

This fennel, radicchio and Gorgonzola salad from the Treviso region of Italy is ideal for an elegant appetiser.

2 fennel bulbs
1 head radicchio
100 g (4 oz) roughly chopped walnuts
175 g (6 oz) diced Gorgonzola

for the dressing:
6 tbsp olive oil
2 tbsp lemon juice
2 tbsp white balsamic vinegar
1 tbsp honey
½ bunch fresh parsley, roughly chopped
salt and freshly ground pepper

Cut off the fennel leaves and reserve for the garnish. Wash the bulbs, remove the hard core and cut the bulbs into thin strips. Put into a serving bowl. Wash and trim the radicchio, shred it (not too finely) and add to the bowl. Add the chopped walnuts and diced Gorgonzola to the bowl.

Make a dressing from the oil, lemon juice, vinegar, honey and parsley. Season to taste with salt and pepper.

Just before serving, pour the dressing over the salad and mix well. Serve immediately, garnished with the fennel leaves.

Serves 4

asian slaw

see variations page 191

If you like Asian flavours, you'll especially enjoy this light, crisp salad with its sweet-sharp ginger and sesame dressing.

2 carrots
450 g (1 lb) shredded green cabbage
450 g (1 lb) shredded red cabbage
½ bunch fresh Thai basil

for the dressing:
2 tbsp sesame seeds
1 tbsp brown sugar
1 tsp freshly grated ginger
1 tbsp sesame oil
1 tsp sesame paste
juice of 1 lime
1 chilli pepper, finely chopped

Peel and shred the carrots, using a mandoline vegetable slicer if available. Put the carrots into a large serving bowl with the shredded cabbage.

To make the dressing, mix the sesame seeds with the brown sugar, grated ginger, sesame oil and paste, lime juice and finely chopped chilli.

Mix the dressing with the shredded cabbage and carrots and leave to stand for about 15 minutes. Mix in the chopped Thai basil just before serving.

Serves 4

variations

carrot salad with pearl onions & parsley

see base recipe page 173

carrot salad with pearl onions, parsley & poppy seeds

Prepare the basic recipe, sprinkling ½ tablespoon poppy seeds over the salad with the vinegar.

spicy carrot & pearl onion salad

Prepare the basic recipe, adding ½ finely chopped, deseeded red chilli pepper to the pan with the carrots.

carrot & leek salad

Prepare the basic recipe, using 2 sliced leeks in place of the pearl onions.

carrot, yellow pepper & pearl onion

Prepare the basic recipe, adding 2 deseeded, sliced yellow peppers to the pan with the carrots.

variations

green papaya & chilli salad

see base recipe page 174

carrot, green papaya & chilli salad
Prepare the basic recipe, using 1 green papaya and 2 large carrots in place of the original 1–2 papayas.

spicy carrot & kohlrabi salad
Prepare the basic recipe, using 2 large carrots and 2 kohlrabi (peeled) in place of the papaya.

spicy green papaya salad with peanuts
Prepare the basic recipe, adding 4 tablespoons roughly chopped peanuts.

green papaya, chilli & chicken salad
Prepare the basic recipe, adding 2 sliced grilled chicken breasts.

green papaya, chilli & prawn salad
Prepare the basic recipe, adding 225 g (8 oz) cooked, peeled and deveined prawns.

variations

two-tone coleslaw

see base recipe page 176

blueberry coleslaw
Prepare the basic recipe, using 3 tablespoons dried blueberries in place of the raisins.

pear coleslaw
Prepare the basic recipe, using 1 firm, ripe pear in place of the apple.

extra-crunchy coleslaw
Prepare the basic recipe, adding 4 stalks sliced celery to the shredded vegetables before dressing.

chicken coleslaw
Prepare the basic recipe, adding 3 diced, grilled chicken breasts to the shredded vegetables before dressing.

pecan coleslaw salad
Prepare the basic recipe, adding a small handful of pecans to the shredded vegetables before dressing.

variations

country slaw

see base recipe page 178

country slaw with honey–mustard dressing
Prepare the basic recipe, whisking 1 teaspoon Dijon mustard into the dressing.

country slaw with dried cranberries
Prepare the basic recipe, adding 3 tablespoons dried cranberries to the prepared vegetables.

country slaw with fresh oranges
Prepare the basic recipe. Cut away the peel from 2 oranges, then slice between the segments to release the flesh to add to the salad.

country slaw with apple
Prepare the basic recipe, adding 1 cored, diced apple to the prepared vegetables.

variations

red cabbage salad with jicama & peppers

see base recipe page 180

red cabbage salad with cucumber & peppers
Prepare the basic recipe, using 1 peeled, deseeded cucumber in place of the jicama.

red cabbage salad with nectarines & peppers
Prepare the basic recipe, using 3 pitted nectarines, cut into bite-sized pieces, in place of the jicama.

red cabbage salad with kohlrabi & peppers
Prepare the basic recipe, using 2 peeled kohlrabi in place of the jicama.

red cabbage salad with daikon & peppers
Prepare the basic recipe, using 1 peeled daikon radish in place of the jicama.

variations

insalata trevigiana

see base recipe page 182

fennel, radicchio & orange salad
Prepare the basic recipe, omitting the Gorgonzola. Instead, cut away the peel and white pith from 3 oranges, then cut between the membranes to remove the flesh. Add the pieces to the salad just before dressing.

fennel, radicchio & goat's cheese salad
Prepare the basic recipe, using diced goat's cheese in place of the Gorgonzola.

fennel, radicchio & peach salad
Prepare the basic recipe, omitting the Gorgonzola. Instead, add 3 pitted nectarines, cut into bite-sized slices, just before serving.

fennel, radicchio & gorgonzola salad with black olives
Prepare the basic recipe, adding 50 g (2 oz) black olives with the Gorgonzola.

fennel, rocket & gorgonzola salad
Prepare the basic recipe, using 2 handfuls of rocket leaves in place of the radicchio.

variations

asian slaw

see base recipe page 184

asian-style slaw with chinese leaves
Prepare the basic recipe, replacing the green and red cabbage with 1 shredded head of Chinese cabbage.

asian slaw with toasted cashews
Prepare the basic recipe, adding a large handful of toasted cashews to the shredded cabbage and carrots.

asian slaw with fresh coriander
Prepare the basic recipe, using a large handful of roughly chopped fresh coriander leaves in place of the Thai basil.

ruby-red asian slaw
Prepare the basic recipe, adding 1 finely shredded beetroot with the shredded cabbage and carrot.

main course salads

A light, healthy salad containing fresh, leafy vegetables, sustaining carbohydrates and essential protein makes a great choice for a main meal. Enjoy for lunch or supper, and if you're feeling extra-hungry, serve with wedges of crusty bread on the side.

salade niçoise

see variations page 217

One of the all-time classic salads, niçoise is an easy midweek family supper as well as suitable for entertaining friends.

150 g (5–6 oz) fresh green beans
1 clove garlic
1 head radicchio, torn into bite-sized pieces
75 g (3 oz) frisée (curly endive), torn into bite-sized pieces
3 spring onions, cut in thin rings
175 g (6 oz) cherry tomatoes, halved
2 hard-boiled eggs, peeled and cut in eighths
175 g (6 oz) tinned white albacore tuna
50 g (2 oz) pitted and halved black olives
for the dressing:
6 tbsp olive oil
juice of 1 lemon
salt and freshly ground pepper

Trim the ends of the beans and cook in plenty of boiling, salted water for 5–6 minutes. Drain, refresh in cold water and drain again.

Rub a large serving bowl with a halved garlic clove. Put the radicchio, frisée, spring onions, tomatoes and eggs into the bowl. Add the drained beans.

Drain and flake the tuna and add to the salad bowl along with the olives. Mix the olive oil and lemon juice to make a dressing and season with salt and pepper. Sprinkle the salad with the dressing and serve.

Serves 4

seafood salad with avocado & peppers

see variations page 218

This fresh, zesty seafood salad is wonderful served on a bed of mixed salad leaves, with buttered wholemeal bread on the side.

400 g (14 oz) cooked prawns
200 g (7 oz) crab meat or surimi (imitation crab), cut into pieces
1 cucumber, halved, seeds removed and diced
2 red peppers, diced
2 avocados, diced

for the dressing:
2 limes
1 tsp brown sugar
3 tbsp olive oil
sea salt and freshly ground pepper
fresh parsley, to garnish

Put the prawns, surimi, cucumber, peppers and avocados into a large serving bowl.

Cut 1 lime into wedges and set aside. Squeeze the other lime into a bowl. Mix the lime juice with the brown sugar and olive oil. Season to taste with sea salt and pepper. Pour the dressing over the salad and toss to combine thoroughly. Leave to stand for about 10 minutes before serving, garnished with parsley and the lime wedges.

Serves 4

taco salad

see variations page 219

Crispy, crunchy tacos are the perfect accompaniment for this spicy Tex-Mex-inspired salad.

400 g (14 oz) minced meat (beef, turkey or your preference)
1 tbsp flour
2 tbsp clarified butter
1 small onion, sliced
1 shallot, sliced
4 ripe tomatoes, diced
1 head crisp lettuce (preferably Batavia or substitute iceberg), torn
1 carrot, julienned, to garnish
grated cheddar cheese, to garnish
taco chips, to serve

for the dressing:
good pinch of chilli powder
175–225 ml (6–8 fl. oz) soured cream
3 tbsp white wine vinegar
salt and pepper

Dust the meat with flour, mix loosely, then fry in clarified butter, breaking it up to brown. Add the sliced onion and shallot and fry briefly. Remove pan from heat, and drain the meat.

Mix all the dressing ingredients, season to taste and put into a bowl. Mix the diced tomatoes with the lettuce and put into individual bowls. Put the meat on top of the lettuce and garnish with the carrot sticks and shredded cheese. Serve with taco chips and the dressing.

Serves 4

rice & pepper salad with grilled chicken breast

see variations page 220

This vibrant yellow salad speckled with red pepper is fragrant and tangy and great for eating at home or for taking to work for lunch at your desk.

450 ml (16 fl. oz) vegetable stock
½ tsp powdered turmeric
225 g (8 oz) long-grain rice
4 tbsp corn or canola oil
2 red peppers, cut in strips
1 ripe tomato, finely diced
4 tbsp freshly squeezed lime juice
salt and pepper
1 chilli pepper
1 tbsp freshly chopped coriander, plus leaves to garnish
3–4 boneless, skinless chicken breasts
2 tbsp sunflower oil (or canola oil)

Pour the vegetable stock into a saucepan and add the turmeric. Bring the stock to the boil. Add the rice, stir, cover the pan and bring the stock back to the boil. Turn the heat down to very low and cook the rice for about 20 minutes, covered (do not lift the lid), until all the liquid is absorbed. Remove the pan from the heat, drain the rice, rinse with cold water and put into a large salad bowl.

Heat a little corn oil in a frying pan and sauté the peppers and tomato. Add to the salad bowl.

Season the lime juice with salt and pepper. Whisk the rest of the corn oil into the seasoned lime juice to make a vinaigrette. Wash the chilli, slit open lengthways, remove the seeds and

white inner ribs and dice finely. Stir into the vinaigrette. Add the dressing to the rice and vegetables and combine. Set aside.

Remove any fat from the chicken breasts, wash, dry and season with pepper. Heat the sunflower oil in a frying pan and fry the chicken on both sides for about 5 minutes, or until cooked through. Remove from the pan. When cool enough to handle, slice the breasts at an angle.

Spoon the rice salad onto individual plates, top with chicken slices and serve, garnished with coriander.

Serves 4

tuna salad with grilled tomatoes & rocket

see variations page 221

Nutty, peppery rocket is a wonderful base for sweet, tender, grilled tomatoes and tuna in this light, flavoursome salad.

550 g (1¼ lb) small–medium ripe tomatoes, halved crossways
2 red onions, cut in wedges
small bunch fresh herbs (parsley, lemon balm, oregano, rosemary, sage and thyme), finely chopped
1 dried red chilli pepper, finely chopped
5 tbsp olive oil
salt and pepper
4 tbsp aged balsamic vinegar
2 x 185-g (6½-oz) tins tuna, drained and flaked
1 bunch rocket

Put the tomatoes and onions, cut-sides up, on a baking tray lined with parchment paper or waxed paper. In a bowl, mix the herbs with the chilli and half of the olive oil. Season with salt and pepper. Sprinkle the herb–chilli mixture over the tomatoes, then grill for 7–10 minutes, watching carefully so they do not burn. Remove and set aside.

Mix the rest of the olive oil with the vinegar and season lightly with salt and pepper. Arrange a bed of rocket on each plate. Arrange the flaked tuna, tomatoes and onions on the rocket. Sprinkle the dressing over each salad and serve.

Serves 4

mixed salad with diced tofu & parmesan

see variations page 222

Tofu is a great source of vegetarian protein, making this salad an ideal choice for anyone following a meat-free diet.

350 g (12 oz) tofu
3 tbsp soy sauce
2 tbsp apple cider vinegar
2 tbsp soybean oil (or canola)
2 good pinches freshly ground pepper
400 g (14 oz) tomatoes, cut into eighths
450 g (1 lb) mixed lettuce leaves, torn
1 small white onion, diced
25 g (1 oz) Parmesan, to garnish

Cut the tofu into 1-cm (½-inch) cubes and put into a bowl. Add the soy sauce, vinegar and 1 tablespoon soya oil. Sprinkle with pepper and mix well. Marinate the tofu for about 10 minutes, stirring occasionally.

Put the tomatoes and lettuce leaves into a serving bowl and pour the marinade from the tofu over them.

Heat the rest of the oil in a frying pan over medium heat. Sauté the diced tofu, turning frequently. Add the onion at the end and sauté briefly. Mix the tofu and onion with the tomatoes and lettuce. Shave the Parmesan over the salad with a vegetable peeler, and serve.

Serves 4

spinach salad with lamb

see variations page 223

Tender, juicy lamb is especially sweet and succulent with leafy salads, particularly those made with dark green spinach leaves.

275 g (10 oz) lamb loin fillet
2 tbsp oil for frying
salt and pepper
275 g (10 oz) baby spinach leaves, torn
½ head frisée (curly endive), torn
1 red onion, sliced
½ bunch fresh chives, to garnish

for the dressing
½ shallot, finely chopped
1 clove garlic, finely chopped
4 tbsp sherry vinegar
½ tsp mustard
1 tsp honey
6–8 tbsp olive oil

Heat the oil for frying in a frying pan and quickly sauté the lamb fillet on both sides over a fairly high heat. Season with salt and pepper, reduce the heat and fry for an additional 5 minutes. Wrap in aluminium foil and leave to rest in a very low oven for 5–8 more minutes.

To make the dressing, put the shallot, garlic, vinegar, mustard, honey and olive oil into a deep bowl and whisk. Toss the spinach, frisée and onion with the vinaigrette. Thinly slice the lamb fillet. Arrange the lamb slices and salad leaves on plates, alternating the lamb and greens. Garnish with chives before serving.

Serves 4

carpaccio with parmesan & rocket

see variations page 224

Wafer-thin slices of marinated raw beef are an Italian classic known as carpaccio. They're delicious as a salad with peppery rocket leaves and scented porcini oil.

300 g (11 oz) beef tenderloin
juice of 1 lemon, squeezed
salt and freshly ground pepper
6 tbsp porcini oil (from delicatessen)
Parmesan cheese, to serve
rocket, to serve

Wrap the beef tenderloin in clingfilm and freeze for about 20 minutes. Slice into wafer-thin slices with a sharp knife. Put each slice between sheets of clingfilm and pound carefully and evenly with the flat side of a meat mallet. Arrange beef on 4 well-chilled plates.

Mix the lemon juice and salt, then whisk in the oil. Sprinkle the dressing over the carpaccio and season with freshly ground pepper. Scatter with fine Parmesan shavings and rocket leaves.

Serves 4

salmon fillet on potato & mangetout salad

see variations page 225

This warm salmon salad with new potatoes, mangetout and cherry tomatoes makes an elegant and colourful meal for two – perfect for no-fuss romancing.

450 g (1 lb) small potatoes
275 g (10 oz) mangetout
225 g (8 oz) cherry tomatoes, halved
I clove garlic
1 red chilli pepper
1 bunch fresh basil, plus a few leaves for garnish
2 tbsp white wine vinegar
6 tbsp olive oil, plus more for brushing
salt and freshly ground pepper
2 pieces salmon fillet, each weighing about 150–175 g (5–6 oz)

Wash the potatoes well and cook in salted water until tender. Drain, leave to steam dry and halve. Top and tail the mangetout and blanch in boiling, salted water for 4 minutes. Drain well. Put the potatoes and peas into a large bowl. Add the tomatoes and toss together.

Peel and roughly chop the garlic. Wash, deseed and finely chop the chilli. Wash the basil and shake dry. In a blender or food processor, purée the basil with the garlic, chilli, vinegar and olive oil. Season with salt and pepper. Pour the dressing over the potatoes, peas and tomatoes and leave to stand for a while.

Brush the salmon with a little oil, season with salt and pepper and cook on a grill (not too hot) for 2–3 minutes per side.

Arrange the potato salad on individual plates. Top each serving with a salmon fillet and garnish with basil leaves.

Serves 2

chicken salad with spinach & papaya

see variations page 226

Sweet-scented papaya and smooth buttery avocado are a wonderful combination in this simple, leafy chicken salad, which makes a fabulous dish for lunch or supper.

2 tbsp vegetable oil
2 boneless, skinless chicken breasts (about 200 g/ 7 oz each)
1 ripe avocado
1 tbsp lemon juice
1 ripe papaya
275 g (10 oz) fresh spinach, in bite-sized pieces
1/4 head iceberg lettuce, in bite-sized pieces
1 red onion, sliced into rings

for the dressing:
2–3 tbsp butter
2 tbsp fennel seeds
1 level tsp sugar
50 ml (2 fl. oz) white balsamic vinegar
salt and freshly ground pepper

Heat the vegetable oil in a frying pan, add the chicken breasts and cook on both sides for about 7 minutes, until cooked through. Whilst the chicken is cooking, make the fennel seed dressing. Melt the butter in a pan, add the fennel seeds and heat for 1–2 minutes, then sprinkle with sugar and heat until lightly caramelised. Stir in the balsamic vinegar and remove from the stove.

Halve the avocado, remove the stone, cut the fruit into wedges and remove the skin. Slice the avocado wedges and sprinkle with lemon juice. Peel and halve the papaya and remove the seeds. Cut the fruit into bite-sized pieces. Place the spinach, lettuce, onion, avocado and papaya into a large salad bowl. Slice the chicken (either warm or cold) thinly and toss with the salad ingredients. Sprinkle with the fennel seed dressing.

Serves 4

lobster, grapefuit & avocado salad with beetroot

see variations page 227

Tangy grapefruit, creamy avocado and glorious magenta-coloured beetroot offer the perfect partnership with sweet, succulent lobster in this luxurious salad.

100 ml (4 fl. oz) white wine
1 Hamburg parsley root, roughly diced
1 stalk celery, roughly diced
1 carrot, roughly diced
1 onion, roughly diced
3 stalks parsley
1 bay leaf
2 sprigs thyme
salt and freshly ground pepper
1 lobster (approximately 800 g/1¾ lb)

for the salad:
1 beetroot (approx. 100 g/ 4 oz)
3 tbsp grapeseed oil (or canola oil)
juice of ½ lemon
1 grapefruit
1 avocado
50 g (2 oz) bite-sized or mixed salad leaves (such as radicchio, rocket, spinach)
sea salt

In a large pot, place 700 ml (2¼ fl. oz) water and the white wine. Bring to the boil. Add the parsley root, celery, carrot, onion and herbs. Season with salt and pepper and simmer for about 15 minutes. Plunge the lobster, head first, into the broth and cook for 8–10 minutes, depending on size. Take out and refresh in cold water. Cut the lobster in half lengthways with a large, sharp knife. Remove the meat from the tail and the claws. Halve the tail.

To make the salad, steam the beetroot until tender, 25–30 minutes. Cool, peel and dice. Mix with 1 tablespoon oil and 1 tablespoon lemon juice. Peel the grapefruit with a sharp knife, removing the white pith and skin, and cut out the segments. Peel and halve the avocado, remove the seed and cut the flesh into wedges.

Arrange the avocado and grapefruit attractively (like the petals of a flower) on 2 plates, alternating avocado and grapefruit segments. Put a handful of salad leaves in the middle and scatter the diced beetroot around the outside. Put a lobster claw and half of the tail on each plate. Mix the rest of the lemon juice and oil and drizzle it over the salad. Sprinkle with sea salt before serving.

Serves 2

broccoli & cauliflower salad with roquefort dressing

see variations page 228

Blue cheese is a natural partner for broccoli and cauliflower. It's particularly delicious in this creamy, piquant dressing.

400 g (14 oz) broccoli florets
400 g (14 oz) cauliflower florets
225 g (8 oz) radishes, quartered
175 g (6 oz) frisée (curly endive), in bite-sized pieces
400 g (14 oz) halved cherry tomatoes

for the dressing:
50 g (2 oz) Roquefort cheese
5 tbsp cream
5 tbsp natural yoghurt
2 tbsp white balsamic vinegar
salt and freshly ground pepper

Cook the broccoli and cauliflower in boiling, salted water for about 3 minutes, refresh in cold water, then drain.

To make the dressing, mash the Roquefort with a fork, then mix with the cream, yoghurt and balsamic vinegar. Season to taste with salt and pepper.

Combine the broccoli, cauliflower, radishes, frisée and tomatoes. Arrange the salad on serving plates. Spoon the dressing over the salad before serving.

Serves 4

chopped ham salad

see variations page 229

This hearty salad containing greens, apple, carrot, ham, nuts and cheese is a great choice for a simple weekday lunch or supper.

1 apple
2 tbsp lemon juice
½ head radicchio, torn
½ head oak-leaf lettuce, torn
½ peeled, diced, deseeded cucumber
1 grated carrot
1 tbsp balsamic vinegar
1 tbsp grapeseed oil (or canola oil)
1 shallot, diced
100 g (4 oz) ham, diced
2 tbsp chopped fresh parsley
2 tbsp chopped walnuts
50 g (2 oz) grated cheddar cheese
salt

Dice the apple and mix it with the lemon juice. Put the apple, radicchio, lettuce, cucumber and carrot into a salad bowl. Add the vinegar, oil, diced shallot, ham, parsley, walnuts and cheese. Mix carefully, season to taste with salt and serve immediately.

Serves 2

variations

salade niçoise

see base recipe page 193

smoked mackerel niçoise
Prepare the basic recipe, using 2 skinned and flaked smoked mackerel fillets in place of the tuna.

fresh tuna niçoise
Prepare the basic recipe, omitting the tinned tuna. Instead, season 2 fresh tuna steaks, squeeze a little lemon juice over them and sear in a very hot pan for about 1 minute on each side. Slice the tuna and arrange on top of the salad.

veggie niçoise
Prepare the basic recipe, omitting the tuna and using 4 hard-boiled eggs instead of 2.

smoked trout niçoise
Prepare the basic recipe, using 2 flaked smoked trout fillets in place of the tuna.

variations

seafood salad with avocado & pepper

see base recipe page 194

prawn salad with avocado & pepper
Prepare the basic recipe, using 550 g (1¼ lb) cooked prawns in place of the original prawns and crab or surimi.

spicy wasabi salad with avocado & pepper
Prepare the basic recipe, whisking ¼–½ teaspoon wasabi paste into the dressing, according to your taste preference.

crab salad with avocado & pepper
Prepare the basic recipe, using 2 tins white crabmeat in place of the prawns and crab or surimi.

zesty chicken salad with avocado & pepper
Prepare the basic recipe, using 4 sliced, grilled chicken breasts in place of the prawns and crab or surimi.

taco salad

see base recipe page 196

spicy tortilla salad
Prepare the basic recipe, serving the salads with soft flour tortillas in place of the taco chips.

taco salad with avocado
Prepare the basic recipe, adding 2 peeled, pitted, diced avocados with the tomatoes and lettuce.

spicy bean taco salad
Prepare the basic recipe, adding 1 x 400-g (14-oz) tin kidney beans, drained and rinsed, with the tomatoes and lettuce.

taco salad with sweet peppers
Prepare the basic recipe, adding 2 deseeded, diced red peppers with the onion and shallot.

variations

rice & pepper salad with grilled chicken breast

see base recipe page 198

rice, pepper & pea salad with grilled chicken breast
Prepare the basic recipe, adding 225 g (8 oz) thawed frozen peas to the salad bowl with the peppers.

rice & pepper salad with ham
Prepare the basic recipe, omitting the chicken. Instead, add 225 g (8 oz) diced smoked ham to the salad with the peppers and tomatoes.

rice & pepper salad with grilled turkey
Prepare the basic recipe, using 3 turkey steaks in place of the chicken.

rice & pepper salad with tuna
Prepare the basic recipe, omitting the chicken breasts. Instead, top the salad with 2 x 185-g (6½-oz) tins tuna, drained and flaked.

rice & green pepper salad with chicken
Prepare the basic recipe, using green peppers in place of red.

variations

tuna salad with grilled tomatoes & rocket

see base recipe page 200

grilled tomato & rocket salad with parmesan
Prepare the basic recipe, omitting the tuna and scattering 25 g (1 oz) grated or flaked Parmesan over the top of the salad before serving.

grilled tomato & rocket salad with chicken
Prepare the basic recipe, omitting the tuna. Scatter 3 sliced, grilled chicken breasts over the salad before serving.

grilled tomato & rocket salad with prosciutto
Prepare the basic recipe, omitting the tuna. Instead, snip 8 strips of prosciutto into bite-sized pieces and scatter them over the salad before serving.

grilled tomato & rocket salad with blue cheese & pine nuts
Prepare the basic recipe, omitting the tuna. Instead, scatter 175 g (6 oz) crumbled Stilton or Roquefort and 3 tablespoons toasted pine nuts over the salad before serving.

variations

mixed salad with diced tofu & parmesan

see base recipe page 202

mixed salad with tofu & apple

Prepare the basic recipe, adding 1 cored, diced apple with the tomatoes and salad leaves.

mixed salad with tofu & green beans

Prepare the basic recipe. Whilst the tofu marinates, boil 200 g (7 oz) trimmed green beans for about 4 minutes until just tender, then refresh under cold water. Add to the salad with the tomatoes and salad leaves.

mixed salad with tofu & bean sprouts

Prepare the basic recipe, adding 2 handfuls of bean sprouts with the tomatoes and lettuce leaves.

mixed salad with ginger-marinated tofu

Prepare the basic recipe, adding 1 teaspoon freshly grated root ginger to the marinade.

mixed salad with spicy chilli tofu

Prepare the basic recipe, adding ¾ deseeded, finely chopped red chilli pepper to the marinade.

variations

spinach salad with lamb

see base recipe page 204

spinach & lamb salad with balsamic dressing
Prepare the basic recipe, using balsamic vinegar in place of sherry vinegar.

spinach & lamb salad with spiced garlic dressing
Prepare the basic recipe, using 1 teaspoon harissa paste in place of the mustard.

spinach & lamb salad pittas
Prepare the basic recipe, and serve inside 4 warmed pitta breads with extra salad on the side.

spinach & lamb salad with tomato
Prepare the basic recipe, adding 275 g (10 oz) halved cherry tomatoes to the salad leaves.

variations

carpaccio with parmesan & rocket

see base recipe page 206

carpaccio with rocket & tomato salad
Prepare the basic recipe, arranging 225 g (8 oz) halved cherry tomatoes on the plates with the rocket and Parmesan.

carpaccio with fragrant salad leaves
Prepare the basic recipe, using a mixed herb salad in place of the rocket.

carpaccio with bitter salad leaves & pear
Prepare the basic recipe, using 3 heads chicory (divided into leaves) in place of the rocket, and arranging 2 sliced pears on the plates with the chicory and Parmesan.

carpaccio with rocket & avocado salad
Prepare the basic recipe, arranging 2 pitted, peeled, sliced avocado on the plates with the rocket and Parmesan.

variations

salmon fillet on potato & mangetout salad

see base recipe page 208

trout, potato & mangetout salad
Prepare the basic recipe, using trout fillets in place of the salmon fillets.

smoked mackerel, potato & mangetout salad
Prepare the basic recipe, omitting the salmon. Instead, top each salad with a peppered, smoked mackerel fillet.

poached egg, potato & mangetout salad
Prepare the basic recipe, omitting the salmon. Instead, poach 2 eggs in barely simmering water for 4 minutes, then drain well and gently place one on each salad.

salmon, potato & green bean salad
Prepare the basic recipe, using 225 g (8 oz) trimmed green beans in place of the mangetout.

salmon, potato, pea & caper salad
Prepare the basic recipe, whisking 1 tablespoon roughly chopped capers into the dressing.

variations

chicken salad with spinach & papaya

see base recipe page 210

chicken salad with rocket & mango
Prepare the basic recipe using rocket in place of the spinach, and 1 ripe mango in place of the papaya.

chicken salad with spinach & kiwi
Prepare the basic recipe using 3 peeled kiwi fruit cut into bite-sized pieces, in place of the papaya.

chicken salad with spinach & carrot
Prepare the basic recipe, omitting the papaya. Instead, peel and grate 2 large carrots and toss into the salad with the avocado and onion.

chicken salad with rocket & tomatoes
Prepare the salad omitting the papaya and using rocket in place of the spinach. Add scant 225 g (8 oz) halved cherry tomatoes with the avocado and onion.

chicken salad with spinach, tomatoes & mangetout
Prepare the basic recipe, adding 200 g (7 oz) halved cherry tomatoes and large handful mangetout (steamed for 3 minutes, then refreshed under cold water) to the salad with the avocado and onion.

variations

lobster & avocado salad with beetroot

see base recipe page 212

avocado, grapefruit & beetroot salad

Prepare the basic recipe, omitting the lobster (and wine, Hamburg parsley root, celery, carrot, onion, herbs and seasoning for cooking). Dress and serve as a side salad.

simple crab and avocado salad

Prepare the basic recipe omitting the lobster (and wine, carrot, onion, herbs, and seasoning for cooking). Instead, top the salad with 1 x 185-g ($6\frac{1}{2}$-oz) tin white crab meat.

avocado, blood orange, beetroot & lobster salad

Prepare the basic recipe, using 2 blood oranges in place of the grapefruit.

avocado and lobster salad with shallot dressing

Prepare the basic recipe, whisking $\frac{1}{4}$ shallot finely chopped into the dressing before drizzling over the salad.

variations

broccoli & cauliflower salad with roquefort dressing

see base recipe page 214

broccoli & cauliflower salad with fennel dressing
Prepare the basic recipe, omitting the blue cheese dressing. Instead, use the dressing from chicken salad with spinach and papaya (page 211).

broccoli & cauliflower salad with feta dressing
Prepare the basic recipe, using feta cheese in place of the Roquefort.

broccoli, cauliflower & mangetout salad with blue cheese dressing
Prepare the basic recipe, adding 200 g (7 oz) mangetout to the broccoli and cauliflower for the last minute of cooking time.

broccoli & cauliflower salad with quail's eggs & blue cheese dressing
Prepare the basic recipe, adding 12 peeled, hard-boiled quail's eggs before adding the dressing.

variations

chopped ham salad

see base recipe page 216

chopped ham & egg salad
Prepare the basic recipe, spooning the salad onto 2 plates and topping each serving with a quartered hard-boiled egg.

crunchy ham salad
Prepare the basic recipe, adding 2 sticks sliced celery and 1 deseeded, diced green pepper with the other vegetables. Serve sprinkled with a small handful of croûtons.

tropical chopped ham salad
Prepare the basic recipe, adding 3 diced slices canned pineapple in place of the apple.

fragrant chopped ham salad
Prepare the basic recipe, adding a handful of chopped fresh coriander with the parsley.

asian-style salads

Crisp, refreshing, spicy salads are popular throughout Asia. They're delicious served as an accompaniment to Asian-style curries and stir-fries, or as a main meal with rice or noodles. For an Asian-themed meal, they can make a great choice for an starter.

beef salad with thai basil

see variations page 247

Thinly sliced marinated beef makes a great addition to this spicy and fragrant tomato and herb salad. For a main meal, serve it with rice or noodles.

2 tbsp sunflower oil
400 g (14 oz) beef sirloin
1 tbsp honey
2 tbsp soy sauce
1 bunch fresh Thai basil
1 bunch fresh mint
1 tbsp rice vinegar
1 tbsp sesame oil
2 chilli peppers, finely shredded
4 ripe tomatoes, deseeded and sliced
2 spring onions, chopped
2 cloves garlic, finely chopped
2 tbsp light soy sauce, or to taste

Heat the oil in a frying pan and quickly sauté the meat on all sides over a fairly high heat. Remove the meat from the pan. Mix the honey with the soy sauce and brush the meat with the mixture. Now put into a preheated oven 170°C (325°F/Gas mark 3) for 20–30 minutes, until medium-rare. Take out of the oven and leave to cool. Then slice thinly.

Wash the basil and mint and shake dry. Pick the leaves from the stalks. Slice or chop the leaves, if desired.

Mix the rice vinegar with the sesame oil, basil and mint leaves, chilli peppers, tomatoes, spring onions and garlic. Add light soy sauce to taste and mix with the sliced meat. Serve the salad in bowls.

Serves 4

beef with cabbage & courgette salad

see variations page 248

This simple warm salad is great served as part of a selection of Asian-style dishes such as stir-fries or noodle dishes.

1 head of Chinese cabbage
oil for frying
1 courgette, sliced
salt and freshly ground pepper
450 g (1 lb) beef tenderloin, cut into thin strips
2 shallots, cut into rings
1 clove garlic, finely chopped
scant 50 ml (2 fl. oz) sherry
3 tbsp balsamic vinegar
fresh mint and coriander leaves, to garnish

Wash the Chinese cabbage, remove the stalk and finely shred the leaves. Cover each plate with a bed of cabbage leaves.

Heat a little oil in a frying pan and fry the courgette on both sides for about 2 minutes. Season with salt and pepper.

Heat a little oil in another frying pan and sauté the beef strips on both sides for about 1 minute. Take them out of the pan and arrange on the cabbage with the courgette. Sauté the garlic and shallots in the fat left from frying the beef, and add them to the meat. Deglaze the pan with sherry and balsamic vinegar, season with salt and pepper and drizzle over the salad. Serve garnished with mint and coriander leaves.

Serves 4

thai salad with squid, pork & chilli dressing

see variations page 249

Fragrant and spicy, this salad is terrific for lunch or supper. It's particularly good served with steamed rice or coconut rice.

400 g (14 oz) pork fillet
400 g (14 oz) squid
1 tbsp corn oil
2 cloves garlic, sliced
2 finely chopped chilli peppers
4 tbsp rice wine
175–225 ml (6–8 fl. oz) chicken stock
1 tsp honey
1 tsp finely grated fresh root ginger
2 tbsp light soy sauce, plus more to taste
2 shallots, thinly sliced
2 tbsp rice vinegar
1 tbsp sesame oil
1 tbsp chopped fresh mint, to garnish
1 tbsp chopped fresh coriander, to garnish

Cut the pork into thin strips and squid into scored bite-sized pieces.

Heat the corn oil in a large frying pan. Sauté the garlic for a few minutes. Add the chopped chilli peppers and cook briefly. Pour in the rice wine and chicken stock and deglaze the pan. Add the honey, ginger and 2 tablespoons soy sauce. Stir, then add the strips of pork and squid. Cover and cook gently over a very low heat for just a few minutes; watch that the squid does not get rubbery. Put the mixture into a serving bowl.

Mix together the shallots, rice vinegar and sesame oil, then pour this dressing into the serving bowl. Toss to combine. Leave the salad to cool. Before serving, season again with soy sauce and garnish with a sprinkling of mint and coriander.

Serves 4

sweet & sour cucumber & onion salad with chilli

see variations page 250

Honey, chilli and cider vinegar make an irresistibly tangy dressing for this light and refreshing salad. Serve as an accompaniment to an Asian-style meal or with grilled fish or chicken on a hot summer night.

1 cucumber
1 red onion, sliced lengthways
4 tbsp apple cider vinegar
2 tbsp canola oil
1 tbsp honey
1 dried chilli pepper, crushed
salt

Peel the cucumber, halve lengthways, scrape out the seeds and slice the cucumber. Put into a bowl with the sliced onion, cider vinegar, oil and honey. Toss to mix. Add the crushed chilli pepper, season to taste with salt and serve.

Serves 2

egg noodle salad with sesame chicken & mangetout

see variations page 251

This main meal salad is delicious warm or cold. Try taking it to work for lunch or to a picnic.

550 g (1 1/4 lb) carrot sticks
550 g (1 1/4 lb) halved mangetout
200 g (7 oz) Chinese egg noodles
salt and freshly ground pepper
4 boneless, skinless chicken breasts (approx. 550 g/1 1/4 lb)
4 tbsp oil
2–3 tbsp sesame seeds
2 tsp freshly grated root ginger
100 ml (4 fl. oz) vegetable stock
75 ml (3 fl. oz) soy sauce
2 tbsp white wine vinegar
1 tsp sambal oelek chilli paste
pinch of sugar

Blanch the carrots and mangetout in boiling, salted water for about 3 minutes, then drain, refresh in cold water and drain well. Cook the noodles according to the packet instructions, then drain, refresh in cold water and drain well.

Season the chicken breasts with salt and pepper. Heat 2 tablespoons oil in a large frying pan and fry the chicken breasts for about 5 minutes on each side. Sprinkle with sesame seeds and toss a few times to coat on all sides. When cooked, remove from the pan.

Mix the ginger with the stock, soy sauce, the remaining 2 tablespoons oil, vinegar, sambal oelek and sugar. Mix the dressing with the noodles and vegetables in a large bowl. Slice the chicken. Serve the salad in individual bowls with the sliced chicken on top.

Serves 4

asian noodle salad

see variations page 252

Garlic, ginger, spring onions and fresh Thai basil come together in this simple salad to create an aromatic, fragrant Asian-style flavour.

400 g (14 oz) Chinese egg noodles
275 g (10 oz) fresh green beans
oil for frying
2 cloves garlic, finely chopped
1 tsp freshly grated root ginger
1 bunch spring onions, chopped into rings
350 g (12 oz) shredded bok choy
175–225 ml (6–8 fl. oz) chicken stock
275 g (10 oz) sliced shiitake mushrooms
1 bunch fresh Thai basil, roughly chopped
light soy sauce
ground chilli pepper

Cook the noodles according to the packet instructions until al dente. Drain, refresh in cold water and drain again. Wash and trim the beans and blanch in boiling, salted water for 3–4 minutes. Drain, refresh in cold water and cut into pieces.

Heat a little oil and sauté the beans, garlic and root ginger. Add the spring onions and bok choy and sauté briefly. Add the stock and cook for about 20 minutes. The liquid should almost completely evaporate. Add the mushrooms about 5 minutes before the end of the cooking time. Stir in the noodles and basil, add soy sauce and chilli pepper to taste and serve.

Serves 4

vermicelli salad

see variations page 253

Fine vermicelli noodles make a fabulous base for salads. They are wonderful here, dressed in a ginger and sesame dressing scented with fresh herbs.

scant 450 g (1 lb) packet vermicelli
350 g (12 oz) mangetout
1 tbsp sesame oil
1 tsp freshly grated root ginger
2 tbsp rice vinegar
175 g (6 oz) sliced radishes
200 g (7 oz) oz baby corn
light soy sauce
1 bunch fresh Thai basil, roughly chopped
2 tbsp snipped chives

Cook the vermicelli according to the package instructions. Drain, refresh in cold water and drain again.

Wash and trim the mange tout and blanch in boiling, salted water for about 1–2 minutes. Drain, refresh in cold water and drain again.

Mix the sesame oil with the ginger and vinegar. Add the mangetout, radishes, baby corn and vermicelli. Toss to combine. Add soy sauce to taste. Leave to stand for about 10 minutes, then sprinkle with the Thai basil and chives and serve.

Serves 4

chicken & prawn salad with vegetables & noodles

see variations page 254

This lightly spiced, fragrant salad packed with chicken, prawns, noodles and tender vegetables makes a great choice as a main dish salad.

1 boneless, skinless chicken breast
1 carrot
1 red pepper
100 g (4 oz) mangetout
2 spring onions
1 clove garlic
1 tbsp sesame oil
100 g (4 oz) bean sprouts
1 tbsp freshly grated root ginger
100 g (4 oz) peeled and deveined prawns
50–100 g (2–4 oz) Chinese egg noodles
1 tbsp sesame seeds, lightly toasted
light soy sauce
chilli sauce

Cut the chicken breast into bite-sized pieces. Peel carrot and cut lengthways into thin slices, then cut the slices into tiny sticks. Cut red pepper into thin strips. Blanch the mangetout for about 2 minutes in boiling salted water, then place immediately in cold water to stop the cooking process. Drain well. Chop the spring onions into small pieces. Finely chop the garlic. Set aside until ready to cook.

Heat the oil in a large frying pan. Add the chicken breast pieces and stir-fry. After about 2 minutes, add the carrot sticks and red pepper, stir-fry for another couple of minutes and finally add the mangetout, spring onions, garlic, bean sprouts, ginger and prawns.

Stir-fry everything for about 6 minutes until cooked but still a little crisp. Add the Chinese egg noodles, toss around a little and then mix in the lightly toasted sesame seeds. Season with soy sauce and chilli sauce and serve.

Serves 2

tuna sashimi salad

see variations page 255

Delicate slices of raw tuna are delicious served on top of this Japanese-inspired salad, which is redolent of Asian flavours.

150 g (5 oz) vermicelli
2 tbsp butter
½ small onion, thinly sliced lengthways
6 tbsp dark soy sauce
1 tbsp oyster sauce
2.5 cm (1 in) piece fresh root ginger, finely grated
1–2 tsp rice vinegar
pinch of sugar
300 g (11 oz) very fresh tuna fillet
1 bunch rocket, washed
2 tsp black sesame seeds, to garnish
½ lime, sliced, to garnish

Soak the vermicelli in plenty of lukewarm water according to packet directions. Drain the noodles and cut into smaller pieces with scissors if desired.

Heat 1 tablespoon butter in a frying pan and sauté the onion until translucent. Remove the onion and set aside. Heat the rest of the butter in the pan, add the soy sauce and oyster sauce and boil to reduce slightly. Stir in the ginger and rice vinegar, and add sugar to taste.

Cut the tuna into 6 neat slices.

Put the vermicelli and onions on 2 plates and sprinkle with the soy sauce and ginger dressing. Top with the rocket and arrange 3 slices of tuna on top of each serving. Sprinkle with sesame seeds and garnish with lime slices before serving.

Serves 2

variations

beef salad with thai basil

see base recipe page 231

beef salad with tomatoes, cucumber & thai basil
Prepare the basic recipe, adding ½ cucumber, sliced lengthways, deseeded and sliced, with the tomatoes.

beef salad with tomatoes, bean sprouts & thai basil
Prepare the basic recipe, adding 3 handfuls of mung bean sprouts with the tomatoes.

beef salad with tomatoes, carrots & thai basil
Prepare the basic recipe, adding 2 grated carrots with the tomatoes.

beef salad with thai basil & peanuts
Prepare the basic recipe, sprinkling 3 tablespoons roughly chopped peanuts over the finished salad.

variations

beef with cabbage & courgette salad

see base recipe page 232

ginger beef, cabbage & courgette salad

Prepare the basic recipe, sautéing 1 teaspoon grated fresh ginger with the garlic and shallot.

beef, cabbage & courgette salad with wasabi

Prepare the basic recipe, stirring 1/4 teaspoon wasabi paste into the sherry and balsamic vinegar mixture.

beef, cabbage & courgette salad with spring onions

Prepare the basic recipe, sprinkling the finished salad with 3 finely sliced spring onions.

spicy beef, cabbage & courgette salad

Prepare the basic recipe, adding 1 sliced, deseeded red chilli pepper to the garlic and shallots a minute before the end of cooking time.

variations

thai salad with squid, pork & chilli dressing

see base recipe page 234

thai salad with squid, pork, bean sprouts & chilli dressing
Prepare the basic recipe, tossing 2 large handfuls of mung bean sprouts into the salad just before serving.

thai salad with pork & prawns & chilli dressing
Prepare the basic recipe, omitting the squid. Add 400 g (14 oz) raw, peeled and deveined tiger prawns to the pork about 2 minutes before the end of cooking time. Toss over the heat until the prawns are pink and the pork is cooked through.

sesame thai salad with squid, pork & chilli dressing
Prepare the basic recipe. To serve, toast 2 tablespoons sesame seeds in a dry frying pan for a minute or two until golden, then sprinkle them over the salad.

cashew thai salad with squid, pork & chilli dressing
Prepare the basic recipe, scattering a handful of toasted cashews over the salad just before serving.

thai salad with squid, pork, chinese cabbage & chilli dressing
Prepare the basic recipe. To serve, shred a Chinese cabbage and divide among 4 plates, then spoon the salad on top.

variations

sweet & sour cucumber & onion salad with chilli

see base recipe page 236

sweet & sour cucumber & onion salad with chilli & coriander
Prepare the basic recipe, adding a small handful of fresh coriander with the chilli.

sweet & sour cucumber & onion salad with chilli & basil
Prepare the basic recipe, adding a small handful of torn fresh basil leaves with the chilli.

sweet & sour cucumber & onion salad with chives
Prepare the basic recipe, adding 1 tablespoon snipped fresh chives in place of the chilli.

sweet & sour cucumber, tomato & onion salad with chilli
Prepare the basic recipe, adding 2 ripe tomatoes cut into bite-sized pieces with the cucumber.

sweet & sour cucumber, pear & onion salad with chilli
Prepare the basic recipe, adding 2 thinly sliced peeled, cored pears with the cucumber.

variations

egg noodle salad with sesame chicken & mangetout

see base recipe page 238

egg noodle salad with sesame prawns & mangetout
Prepare the basic recipe, using 275 g (10 oz) raw, shelled, deveined large prawns instead of the chicken. Fry them for 2–3 minutes until pink and cooked through before sprinkling them with the sesame seeds.

egg noodle salad with sesame chicken & broccoli
Prepare the basic recipe, using 225 g (8 oz) fresh broccoli florets in place of the mangetout.

egg noodle salad with sesame chicken & cauliflower
Prepare the basic recipe, using 225 g (8 oz) fresh cauliflower florets in place of the mangetout.

egg noodle salad with sesame chicken, mangetout, & spring onions
Prepare the basic recipe, sprinkling the salad with 5 sliced spring onions before dressing.

egg noodle salad with sesame chicken & green peppers
Prepare the basic recipe, omitting the mangetout. Instead, add 2 sliced, deseeded green peppers to the noodles and carrots before dressing.

variations

asian noodle salad

see base recipe page 240

asian rice noodle salad
Prepare the basic recipe, using 275 g (10 oz) rice noodles in place of the egg noodles.

asian noodle salad with fresh coriander
Prepare the basic recipe, using fresh coriander in place of the Thai basil.

asian noodle salad with cashews
Prepare the basic recipe, adding 2 handfuls of cashews to the pan with the garlic and ginger.

asian noodle salad with prawns
Prepare the basic recipe, adding 275 g (10 oz) cooked, peeled prawns with the cooked noodles.

asian noodle salad with chicken
Prepare the basic recipe, adding 2 sliced, grilled chicken breasts with the cooked noodles.

variations

vermicelli salad

see base recipe page 243

egg noodle salad with mangetout, baby corn & radishes
Prepare the basic recipe, using egg noodles in place of the rice noodles.

spicy vermicelli salad with fresh chilli
Prepare the basic recipe, adding ½ deseeded, finely chopped red chilli pepper to the dressing.

vermicelli salad with peanuts
Prepare the basic recipe, sprinkling 2 tablespoons chopped peanuts over the top of the finished salad.

vermicelli salad with sweet peppers, baby corn & radishes
Prepare the basic recipe, using 2 deseeded red peppers cut into strips in place of the mangetout. (Do not blanch them; simply use raw.)

vermicelli salad with carrots, baby corn & radishes
Prepare the basic recipe, using 3 carrots sliced into sticks in place of the mangetout.

variations

chicken & prawn salad with vegetables & noodles

see base recipe page 244

seafood salad with vegetables & noodles
Prepare the basic recipe, omitting the chicken. Use 225 g (8 oz) cooked, prepared seafood (such as prawns, mussels and squid) in place of the prawns.

chicken salad with vegetables & noodles
Prepare the basic recipe, using 2 chicken breasts and omitting the prawns.

duck salad with vegetables & noodles
Prepare the basic recipe, using 2 duck breasts in place of the chicken and omitting the prawns.

vegetable noodles with cashews
Prepare the basic recipe, omitting the chicken and prawns. Instead, add 2 handfuls of cashews to the pan with the vegetables.

variations

tuna sashimi salad

see base recipe page 246

tiger prawn noodle salad
Prepare the basic recipe, using 175 g (6 oz) cooked, shelled tiger prawns in place of the tuna.

asian-style crab salad
Prepare the basic recipe, replacing the tuna with tinned white crabmeat.

asian-style tofu salad
Prepare the basic recipe, topping the salad with 175 g (6 oz) marinated deep-fried tofu pieces in place of the tuna.

tuna sashimi salad with pickled ginger
Prepare the basic recipe, sprinkling the finished salad with 1 tablespoon pickled ginger.

tuna sashimi salad with wasabi dressing
Prepare the basic recipe, adding 1/4 teaspoon wasabi paste to the dressing.

fruit salads

Packed with vitamins, fibre and health-giving nutrients, fruit salads can be crisp and juicy or sweet and succulent, but what they all have in common is their incredible versatility. Enjoy them for breakfast or as a healthy dessert or guilt-free snack.

cubed melon

see variations page 273

This mixed melon salad – delightful on a hot summer day – also makes a stunning, healthy dessert for a special dinner party.

4 different varieties of ripe melon (such as watermelon, honeydew, cantaloupe, Galia)
white balsamic vinegar, to sprinkle (optional)

Peel and deseed wedges of each melon and cut the flesh into approximately 1-inch cubes (27 in all).

Assemble the cubes into one large cube, mixing up the different varieties. If you wish, serve sprinkled with a little white balsamic vinegar.

Serves 4

exotic fruit salad

see variations page 274

This fresh fruit salad made with exotic tropical fruits and a zingy lime dressing is the perfect dessert any time.

1 dragon fruit (pitahaya)
1 avocado
12 lychees
1 star fruit (carambola)
2 kiwi fruit
1 Asian pear
1 tbsp brown sugar
juice of 1 lime

Within half an hour of serving, prepare the fruit for the salad. Halve the dragon fruit and cut out balls with a melon baller. Peel and halve the avocado, remove the stone and slice the fruit. Peel the lychees and remove the seeds. Wash and slice the star fruit. Peel and slice the kiwis. Wash, halve and core the Asian pear and cut into wedges. Put all the fruit into a serving bowl.

Mix the brown sugar with the lime juice, then mix with the fruit. Leave to stand for about 15 minutes, then serve.

Serves 4

colourful fruit salad with black pepper

see variations page 275

Olive oil and black pepper may sound like odd additions to a fruit salad, but it tastes delicious and really brings out the flavours of the sweet, juicy fruit.

2 dragon fruit (pitahaya)
2 kiwi fruit
8 lychees
1 ripe mango
½ ripe honeydew melon
4 tbsp extra-virgin olive oil
juice of 2–3 limes
freshly ground black pepper
a few cape gooseberries (physalis), to decorate

Cut into the dragon fruit at the top and remove the skin. Halve the fruit lengthways, then cut into large wedges. Peel the kiwis and cut in half. Peel the lychees, halve them and remove the seeds. Peel the mango, remove the seeds and cut into slices. Peel the honeydew melon, remove the seeds and cut into thin slices.

Arrange the fruit decoratively on glass plates or dessert plates. Drizzle olive oil and lime juice over the top. Season with freshly ground pepper, decorate with the cape gooseberries and serve immediately.

Serves 4

mediterranean fruit salad with spices & pistachios

see variations page 276

This simple salad of sweet Mediterranean fruits, sharp grapefruit and warm spices is lovely as a dessert or for a weekend breakfast.

100 g (4 oz) black grapes
2 figs
1 pear
4 dried dates
2 red grapefruit
1 pinch ground cardamom
1 pinch ground cinnamon
juice of 1 lime
1 tbsp chopped pistachios, to decorate

Wash and halve the grapes lengthways and remove the seeds. Cut the figs into bite-sized pieces. Wash the pear, remove the core and cut into slices. Remove the pits from the dates and cut into small pieces. Cut the grapefruit into segments.

Place the cut fruit into a serving bowl. Mix the spices with the freshly squeezed lime juice, then pour the mixture over the fruit. Toss well to combine. Sprinkle with chopped pistachios and serve immediately.

Serves 2

blueberry & papaya salad with toasted almonds

see variations page 277

Try this light, refreshing fruit salad for breakfast with Greek yoghurt and a glass of freshly squeezed fruit juice.

225 g (8 oz) fresh blueberries
2 ripe papayas
100 g (4 oz) blanched almonds
2 tbsp chopped fresh basil leaves
2 tbsp agave syrup (from a health food store) or honey
1 tbsp freshly squeezed lemon juice

Wash and sort the blueberries. Peel and halve the papayas, remove the seeds and dice the flesh. Toast the almonds in a dry frying pan until golden brown, then leave to cool.

Mix the blueberries and diced papaya with the basil, agave syrup and lemon juice. Chill for about 30 minutes. Stir in the toasted almonds shortly before serving.

Serves 4

fruit salad with coconut milk

see variations page 278

The addition of coconut milk gives this fresh, fruity salad a deliciously sweet and creamy flavour. It also makes a great dessert for anyone on a dairy-free diet.

2 blood oranges
1 baby pineapple
1 apple
2 kiwi fruit
1 banana
175 ml (6 fl. oz) unsweetened coconut milk
1 tbsp honey
freshly squeezed lemon juice
seeds from 1 pomegranate
1 tbsp chopped fresh coriander

Peel, halve and slice the blood oranges. Peel, trim and dice the pineapple. Peel, quarter, core and dice the apple. Peel and dice the kiwis. Peel and slice the banana.

In a large serving bowl, mix all the fruit with the coconut milk, honey and lemon juice. Taste and add more honey or lemon if desired. Mix in the pomegranate seeds and coriander and serve.

Serves 4

fig & nectarine salad

see variations page 279

Tender figs and juicy nectarines make a fabulous combination in this cinnamony, rum-spiked salad. Serve it at a dinner party or as a special dessert.

8 figs
3 nectarines
1 tbsp honey
juice of 1 lime
pinch of cinnamon
40 ml (1½ fl. oz) (1 scant jigger) rum

Wash and dry the figs and cut them into slices. Wash the nectarines and cut them in half. Remove the stones and cut into thin wedges. Put the figs and nectarines into a serving bowl.

Mix the lime juice, cinnamon and rum together. Pour the mixture over the fruit, mix thoroughly and leave to marinate for about 10 minutes before serving.

Serves 4

poached fruit compôte

see variations page 280

A cooked fruit compôte makes a wonderful alternative to a fresh fruit salad. It is good served as dessert or at a brunch buffet.

100 g (4 oz) sugar
juice and grated zest of 1 orange
75–100 ml (3–4 fl. oz) port
75–100 ml (3–4 fl. oz) red wine
2 whole cloves
1 cinnamon stick
4 small pears, peeled and halved
4 small peaches, quartered
900 g (2 lb) rhubarb into 4 cm (1½ in) slices
honey, to taste
crushed nut brittle, to decorate

Put the sugar in a saucepan and heat until it caramelises. Stir in the orange juice, port and red wine. Add the cloves, cinnamon stick, orange zest and halved pears. Poach for about 10–15 minutes, then add the peaches and rhubarb. Cover and poach for a further 5 minutes.

With a slotted spoon, remove the fruit from the liquid and set aside. Gently simmer the liquid, stirring occasionally, until it has the consistency of a syrup. Remove the cinnamon stick, cloves and orange zest, and leave the syrup to cool slightly.

Arrange the fruit on plates and add a little of the warm syrup. Drizzle with a little honey, sprinkle with nut brittle and serve.

Serves 4

creamy rice pudding fruit salad

see variations page 281

Sweet and creamy rice pudding makes a rich and luscious base for this fresh and fruity salad.

about 350 ml (12 fl. oz) milk
1 tsp pure vanilla extract
50 g (2 oz) caster sugar
pinch of salt
piece of lemon peel
175 g (6 oz) uncooked pudding rice
2 kiwi fruit, peeled and sliced
350 g (12 oz) fresh raspberries
2 ripe peaches, diced
2 tbsp honey
fresh mint leaves, to decorate

Put the milk into a saucepan with the vanilla extract, sugar, salt and lemon peel. Bring to the boil. Sprinkle in the rice, cover and cook over a low heat for 20–25 minutes, stirring as little as possible. Remove from the heat when all the liquid is absorbed, but the grains of rice are still separate. Leave to cool without a lid.

Prepare the fruit just before serving. Gently mix the cold rice with the fruit and honey. Serve decorated with mint.

Serves 4

variations

cubed melon

see base recipe page 256

cubed melon with ginger
Prepare the basic recipe, sprinkling the melon cubes with ½ teaspoon ground ginger before assembling into a large cube.

cubed melon with mint
Prepare the basic recipe, decorating the melon cube with fresh mint sprigs.

cubed melon with raspberries
Prepare the basic recipe, surrounding the melon cube with 450 g (1 lb) fresh raspberries.

cubed melon with blueberries
Prepre the basic recipe, surrounding the melon cube with 450 g (1 lb) fresh blueberries.

cubed melon with lime
Prepare the basic recipe, tossing the melon cubes in the juice of 1 lime before assembling into a large cube.

variations

exotic fruit salad

see base recipe page 258

pineapple, lychee & dragon fruit salad
Prepare the basic recipe, omitting the avocado, star fruit, kiwi and Asian pear, and instead using 1 fresh pineapple (peeled, cored and eyes removed), cut into bite-sized pieces.

mango, lychee, starfruit & kiwi salad
Prepare the basic recipe, omitting the dragon fruit, avocado and Asian pear, and instead using 2 ripe mangoes (peeled and pitted), cut into bite-sized pieces.

exotic fruit salad with fresh mint
Prepare the basic recipe, sprinkling the fruit with 1 tablespoon chopped fresh mint before dressing.

exotic fruit salad with stem ginger dressing
Prepare the basic recipe, adding 2 chopped pieces stem ginger in syrup to the lime juice mixture.

exotic fruit salad with banana
Prepare the basic recipe, replacing the avocado with 2 peeled, sliced bananas.

variations

colourful fruit salad with black pepper

see base recipe page 260

colourful fruit salad with chilli
Prepare the basic recipe, replacing the black pepper with a pinch of crushed dried chilli flakes.

colourful fruit salad with cinnamon
Prepare the basic recipe, omitting the olive oil and black pepper. Instead, sprinkle the fruit with 1/4 teaspoon ground cinnamon before drizzling with the lime juice; toss to combine.

colourful fruit salad with fresh basil
Prepare the basic recipe, adding a small handful of torn fresh basil leaves to the salad with the lime juice and olive oil.

colourful fruit salad with borage flowers
Prepare the basic recipe, decorating the finished salad with 12 borage flowers.

colourful fruit salad with cucumber
Prepare the basic recipe, omitting the dragon fruit and instead using 1 peeled, deseeded cucumber cut into bite-sized chunks.

variations

mediterranean fruit salad with spices and pistachio nuts

see base recipe page 262

spiced orange & date salad
Prepare the basic recipe, omitting the grapes, figs, pear and grapefruit. Instead, cut away the peel and pith from 4 oranges, then slice and arrange on a serving plate. Sprinkle with the dates, dressing and nuts.

spiced grape, fig & pear salad
Prepare the basic recipe, replacing the grapefruit with 2 extra figs and 1 extra pear.

spiced grape, peach & fig salad
Prepare the basic recipe, omitting the pear, dates and grapefruit. Instead, add 1 extra fig and 2 peeled, pitted peaches cut into bite-sized wedges.

mediterranean fruit salad with spices & walnuts
Prepare the basic recipe, using 2 tablespoons roughly chopped walnuts in place of the pistachio nuts.

variations

blueberry & papaya salad with toasted almonds

see base recipe page 264

raspberry & papaya salad with toasted almonds
Prepare the basic recipe, using raspberries in place of the blueberries.

strawberry & papaya salad with toasted almonds
Prepare the basic recipe, using strawberries (halved or quartered if large) in place of the blueberries.

blueberry & mango salad with toasted almonds
Prepare the basic recipe, using 2 ripe mangoes (peeled and pitted) in place of the papayas.

blueberry & papaya salad with toasted macadamia nuts
Prepare the basic recipe, using macadamia nuts in place of the almonds.

strawberry & mango salad with toasted almonds
Prepare the basic recipe, using strawberries in place of the blueberries and 2 mangoes (peeled and pitted) in place of the papayas.

variations

fruit salad with coconut milk

see base recipe page 266

coconut-topped fruit salad
Prepare the basic recipe, scattering a small handful of toasted coconut flakes over the top of the salad.

spiced fruit salad with coconut milk
Prepare the basic recipe, omitting the coriander. Instead, stir $\frac{1}{4}$ teaspoon ground cinnamon into the coconut mixture.

orange, pineapple & banana salad with coconut milk
Prepare the basic recipe, omitting the apple, kiwi fruit and coriander. Instead, use 1 extra blood orange and 1 extra banana.

coconut fruit salad with star fruit
Prepare the basic recipe, omitting the apple and coriander. Instead, add 2 sliced star fruits in place of the apple.

variations

fig & nectarine salad

see base recipe page 268

fig & peach salad
Prepare the basic recipe, using 6 peeled, pitted peaches in place of the nectarines.

fig & nectarine salad with dates
Prepare the basic recipe, scattering 4 chopped, pitted dates over the salad.

fig & nectarine salad with pistachio nuts
Prepare the basic recipe, sprinkling 2 tablespoons chopped pistachio nuts over the salad.

fig & plum salad
Prepare the basic recipe, using 8 plums in place of the nectarines.

nectarine & plum salad with ginger
Prepare the basic recipe, omitting the honey. Instead, add 1 chopped piece stem ginger and 1 tablespoon syrup from the jar.

fig & nectarine salad with grand marnier
Prepare the basic recipe, using Grand Marnier in place of the rum.

variations

poached fruit compôte

see base recipe page 270

poached fruit compôte with dried apricots
Prepare the basic recipe, using 8 dried apricots with the pears.

poached fruit compôte with figs
Prepare the basic recipe, using 8 halved figs in place of the peaches.

poached fruit compôte with plums
Prepare the basic recipe, using 8 halved, pitted plums in place of the peaches.

poached fruit compôte with slivered almonds
Prepare the basic recipe, scattering 2 tablespoons slivered almonds over the compôte in place of the nut brittle.

poached fruit compôte with star anise
Prepare the basic recipe, using star anise in place of the cinnamon stick.

creamy rice pudding fruit salad

see base recipe page 272

banana & peach salad with rice pudding
Prepare the basic recipe, replacing the kiwi fruit and raspberries with 3 sliced bananas.

fresh berry salad with rice pudding
Prepare the basic recipe, replacing the kiwi fruit and peaches with 225 g (8 oz) strawberries (halved or quartered if large) and 100 g (4 oz) blueberries.

fresh berry & peach salad with rice pudding
Prepare the basic recipe, using 225 g (8 oz) blueberries in place of the kiwi fruit.

spiced rice pudding & fresh fruit salad
Prepare the basic recipe, adding 1 cinnamon stick to the milk and rice. Remove from the rice pudding before cooling.

index